SAND GROWN

The
Lytham St. Annes
Story

by

Kathleen Eyre

LANDY PUBLISHING
1999

ISBN 1 872895 45 X

British Library in Cataloguing Publication Data.
A catalogue record of this book is available from the British Library.

Layout by Mike Clarke using the original format of the fiorst edition of this book, published by Weaver & Youles (Printers) Ltd., Lytham St. Annes, in 1960
01254 395848

This Edition printed by Nayler the Printer Ltd., Accrington
01254 234247

Landy Publishing have also published:

Lancashire, this, that an't'other by Doris Snape
Threads of Lancashire Life by Winnie Bridges
The Really Lancashire Book edited by Bob Dobson
Lancashire Laugh Lines by Kay Davenport
An Accrington Mixture edited by Bob Dobson
A Blackburn Miscellany edited by Bob Dobson
A History of Pilling by F. J. Sobee
Lancashire Lingo Lines edited by Bob Dobson
Rishton Remembered by Kathleen Broderick
Blackburn in Times Gone By by Jim Halsall

A full list is available from:

Landy Publishing
'Acorns' 3 Staining Rise, Staining, Blackpool, FY3 0BU
Tel/Fax: 01253 895678

INTRODUCTION

Landy Publishing are to be congratulated on filling a gap in the all-too-few books about the history of Lytham and the district, with this re-publication of Kathleen Eyre's well researched and delightfully presented book. *Sand Grown* was her first venture into print way back in 1960.

Her untimely death in 1985 denied us of much of what she would have gone on to write. Thankfully, a long string of titles on the subject of her love of the Fylde and of Lancashire and their people is still available to us through public libraries. For those who would treasure a copy of that first book, we now have such an opportunity.

Taken from us at the height of her literary genius, for too long we have been denied being able to savour Kathleen's capacity to furnish the dry bones of history in gorgeously rich raiments, together with her colourful descriptions of the folk of olden days. I am certain that today's readers will savour, as we did (and still do), her descriptive narratives of the history of the locality, and will wish to read more of her talented portrayal of both the Fylde and the wider Lancashire scene.

It is remarkable that I read the proofs for both Kathleen's very first book and also her last (though not all of the very many in between) and I rejoice that only two or three days before her death she was able to see me and discuss the galley proofs of that last book, *Scenes from the Fylde Coast and Country*, which was published by the publishing arm of Lancashire County Library shortly after her demise.

I feel certain that this re-publication will trigger a demand to read more of her works which are still available in public libraries - an impressive list of thirteen books, all on local history and allied subjects.

Thanks are due to the staff of St. Annes Library; to Bill Owen for the use of a photograph of Lytham windmill; to Andrew Firth for the use of photographs from his collection; and to the Lytham Heritage Group for the loan of material. Special thanks to Mrs. Merelyn Eyre Greaves for granting permission to copy and republish her mother's book.

Stanley Brown
Shrimp Cottage
Westby Street
Lytham
March 1999

Kathleen Eyre's Books

Sand Grown (the Story of Lytham St. Annes); Famous Lakeland Homes; Famous Lancashire Homes; Fylde Folk, Moss or Sand; Bygone Blackpool; Chapel in the Dunes (The centenary history of The Drive Methodist Church, St. Annes); Lancashire Ghosts; Lancashire Landmarks; Lancashire Legends; Lytham St. Annes in old picture postcards; The Real Lancashire; Seven Golden Miles (the fantastic story of Blackpool); Witchcraft in Lancashire; Scenes from Fylde Coast & Country.

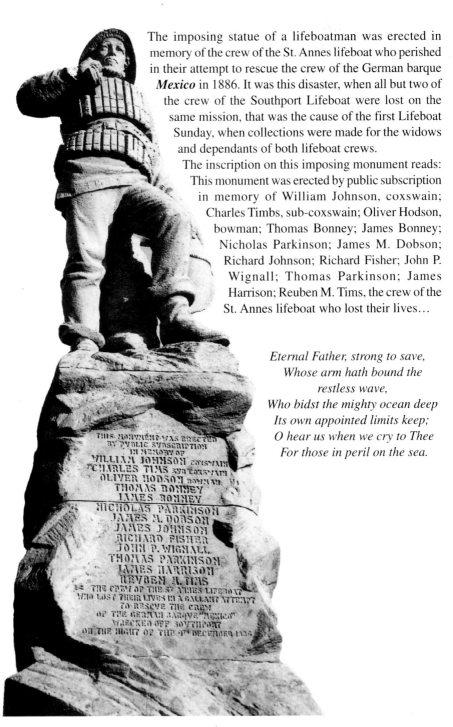

The imposing statue of a lifeboatman was erected in memory of the crew of the St. Annes lifeboat who perished in their attempt to rescue the crew of the German barque ***Mexico*** in 1886. It was this disaster, when all but two of the crew of the Southport Lifeboat were lost on the same mission, that was the cause of the first Lifeboat Sunday, when collections were made for the widows and dependants of both lifeboat crews.

The inscription on this imposing monument reads: This monument was erected by public subscription in memory of William Johnson, coxswain; Charles Timbs, sub-coxswain; Oliver Hodson, bowman; Thomas Bonney; James Bonney; Nicholas Parkinson; James M. Dobson; Richard Johnson; Richard Fisher; John P. Wignall; Thomas Parkinson; James Harrison; Reuben M. Tims, the crew of the St. Annes lifeboat who lost their lives…

Eternal Father, strong to save,
Whose arm hath bound the
restless wave,
Who bidst the mighty ocean deep
Its own appointed limits keep;
O hear us when we cry to Thee
For those in peril on the sea.

CONTENTS

PREFACE

Many years have elapsed since the late " Uncle " Billy Jameson of Leach Lodge Farm, St. Annes, used to sit in my kitchen recalling fascinating tales of the old days.

Fired with curiosity, I began to read, and delve, and ask interminable questions especially of our sand-grown veterans— octogenarians and even nonogenarians as some of them were—who happily, through his introduction, were delighted to sit and chat and let me note down their memories.

In 1950, on the occasion of the 75th birthday of St. Annes, Mr. John Grime, then Editor of the " Lytham-St. Annes Express," accepted and published my first article and, in doing so, pitchforked me into an enthralling way of life for which I can never be grateful enough.

It would be impossible to count the number of hours I have spent in reference libraries, not only within this borough, but at Blackpool, Preston, Manchester and Birmingham. Town Hall officials afforded me facilities for research and over a long period of years bore my queries with the utmost courtesy. The St. Annes librarian, Miss D. Shepherd, not only laid the full resources of the Carnegie Reference Library at my disposal, but went out of her way to help me on every possible occasion.

But there were many more kindly disposed individuals, whether in the borough or beyond it, who welcomed one of the younger generation coming again and again to ask questions about the past. To all these wonderful people, whether named or unnamed, I shall remain everlastingly indebted.

Eventually, I turned, as all local historians must, to the County Records Office, Preston, and discovered there a treasure store of historical documents to which I have returned times without number.

During all this time the thought has plagued me that the memories of the old " sandgrown 'uns " ought to be put on lasting record. Newspaper articles are read, enjoyed perhaps, and thrown away, but a book, however small and inexpensive, stands a chance of surviving into the future. It was a great joy to me, therefore, when a publisher was found for this work which I hope will serve as a helpful guide to visitors, answer many local queries, revive old memories, and preserve the robust reminiscences of a vanished generation.

I have been supported in this task by a host of willing helpers and my gratitude and affection will ever flow out toward them. I would like, very specially, to record my thanks to Mrs. Clifton, not only for contributing a foreword, but for her unfailing interest in my work in recent years, for her patience with my many requests, and for receiving me always with the utmost kindness and courtesy.

My special thanks are also due to J. J. Bagley, Esq., M.A., Staff Tutor in History, Liverpool University, Hon. Editor of the Historic Society of Lancashire and Cheshire. Mr. Bagley taught me how to set my local knowledge into the larger tapestry of county and national history; he broadened my interest, enriched my studies and, in the preparation of this book, came readily to my assistance. Numerous useful amendments have been made at Mr. Bagley's suggestion, and many details have been included which otherwise I might have overlooked. Here and wholeheartedly I acknowledge all his generous help and encouragement.

The many fine illustrations contained in the following pages could not have been brought together without the good will and co-operation of a number of kindly folk. Their contributions have been acknowledged in the appropriate places, but I would like all who have loaned original water colour studies, photographs, prints, blocks, and pictorial matter of whatever sort, to be assured of my warmest thanks and deep appreciation.

Lastly, I would pay tribute to three of my good friends from the St. Annes Branch W.E.A., Mrs. Nora Lawton, Mr. Walter Brayshaw and Mr. Stanley Brown, who assisted in the laborious business of reading the proofs.

To posterity I now bequeath the story of the "sandgrown 'uns" which seemed to me too good to lose, and which afforded me as much joy to compile as it now gives me to see it captured for all time within the covers of this book.

KATHLEEN EYRE.

AUGUST, 1960.   FOUR WINDS FARM, ST. ANNES.

FROM THE BEGINNING . . .

This is not a chronological history of Lytham, but the story of a people. An indomitable breed they were, weather-beaten, wiry, and less than giants. Their forebears lived along this coast from ancient times, and the blood of many races flows in their veins.

They stemmed in the beginning, our natives, from the tribe called Brigantes. Theirs was the Bronze-Age Neolithic culture, and backward they were compared with their Iron Age neighbours further south. But they lived a settled life, had a tribal organisation, and by 51 A.D., when their queen, Cartimandua, handed Caractacus over to the Romans, they had evolved a civilisation of a sort.

Within the shadows of a dark forest reaching down to the sea they lived in tribal groups, bending the branches of trees to form their shelters, waging a never-ending battle against the wild Atlantic elements and the uncertain sea, and leaping amongst the marshlands with their long hair streaming about their shoulders, and clad in woollen clothing and boots made of skin.

Theirs was the continuing struggle to support life in a wild and forgotten corner of the north-west, but theirs also was the desperate courage born of adversity. From long times they had defied the treacherous boglands, and fended off the attacks of marauding animals, but at last the Romans came to mop up this irksome pocket of resistance, and our courageous coastal folk were brought to their knees.

During three and a half centuries they learned a lot from their civilised masters and Christianity was beginning to direct their way of life. When the Roman Empire crashed and the occupying forces withdrew from this island, the natives remained to nurture a mongrel strain.

From 400 to about 600 A.D., these Romano-British lived virtually undisturbed except when their old-time enemies, the Picts and Scots occasionally came swarming, to ravage an unprotected land, and to leave a trail of death and destruction in their wake.

Our coast-folk then were glad of their swamp-ridden woodland in whose darkest recesses they hid again, for very terror, when a new menace appeared from the east.

The Angles had braved the vast stretches of the North Sea in their tiny boats and landed on the other side of the country. Gradually these new intruders eased their way over to the west, spreading their tentacles along the river beds, moving over the high Pennines, and stealing ever nearer to the coast on the west. Clashing or mingling, the two peoples learned how to live together, and by the early years of the seventh century the first Anglian settlements were formed. Thus the blood of the "sandgrown 'uns" was mingled anew.

Again, the centuries rolled by. About the year 900 A.D., once more with anxious eyes they scanned the westerly skyline. Boatloads of Norsemen, Scandinavian by descent, close cousins of the dreaded Danes, were coming in from the Irish settlements of their forefathers to colonise the north-west of England. Christianity, meantime, had cast some softening influence over the invaders, and much of their earlier savagery was spent. This our coastal communities would only learn by degrees, and there would be many a local skirmish before the Norse infiltration was accepted as a non-aggressive invasion.

But peace was still a stranger to the North-West whose overlord, by 1066, was Count Tostig, brother of Saxon King Harold. Tostig's treachery in supporting a false claimant to the English throne cost him his life, and ten days later Harold too, last of the Saxon monarchs, was struck down by the Norman invaders at the Battle of Hastings.

Within a handful of years the whole of the North was reeling under the hammer blows of the new Conqueror's forces. The Norman, with exquisite ruthlessness, ground his heel into the neck of a vanquished nation. Important families were cast out and cottagers put to flight. By 1086, of the 62 old townships of Amounderness, only 16 still supported human life, and how meagrely at that was never recorded.

William's henchman, Roger of Poitou, was now the great overlord of this district, but he in due time fell from favour.

Then came the twelfth century which saw the foundation of so many monastic houses in Lancashire. In 1190, Richard Fitz Roger gave his lands in " Lethum " to the Benedictines at Durham that they might establish a house of their order within the Manor.

Modestly at first, the Priory took shape, starting out, as indeed it finished, with no more than three monks, plus an assortment of secular employees, and gradually expanding in influence and authority until at last we saw them emerge as the supreme arbiters of Lytham's destiny. They were landlords. They were farmers. They kept an eagle eye on the tithes and a firm grip on the community. And from the beginning they were caught up in never-ending feuds over boundaries. In 1443 they severed their dependence upon Durham, and the Compoti show us how skilfully they managed their affairs.

The Dissolution sent them the way of all the others, and bereft of their leadership, the " sandgrown 'uns " were left groping uncertainly through a temporal and spiritual fog. Thomas Dannett, Sir Thomas Holcroft, the Molyneaux family of Sefton, and George and Ellen Rogerly, all in their turn took a hand in the affairs of the parish. But the " sandgrown 'uns " were as sheep without a shepherd, the inhabitants of a manor without a true lord.

In 1606, Cuthbert (later, Sir Cuthbert) Clifton of Westby, bought the estate for £4,300, and thus began a family influence which, unwavering, has reached down over the centuries, until the name of Clifton has become almost synonymous with that of Lytham itself.

So the lordship flourished, preserving its ancient, almost feudal traditions, honouring the Court Leet, cleaving unto the old faith, and going (comparatively) soberly about its business, untouched by the world outside. But for the sea-bathing vogue, so it might have continued through the rest of time, for the " sandgrown 'uns ", reared in poverty, were reconciled to privation.

They worked on the land. They pushed their tiny boats out to sea and dried their nets on the edge of a great water. It was to the Lord of the Manor they looked for their humble accommodation, and from the family at the Hall they took their lead in political and religious affairs.

From the records of the Manor Court, going back to 1504, we find the same names cropping up, and the thread of life continuing down the centuries. Names like Fyssher, Cardewell, Salthowse, Cokeson, Bonny, Symson, Hesketh, Jankynson, Crocowe, Harison, Wright, Wilson . . . and a host of others of which modern counterparts can be found in the district today.

They were largely a law-abiding lot. They might occasionally forget to scour out their ditches ; they might evade the Prior's chapman and sell their catch of fish in Preston, on the sly ; they might help themselves to a tree or two from the lord's estate, cross the lord's pasture with their pigs,

A busy scene in St. Annes Square, looking towards West Crescent at its junction with Park Road with two expensive limousines parked outside the Midland Bank. The cycle rack, bottom left, is outside J. R. Taylor's store, next door to J. H. Taylor's (The Chymist) and the Café Royal, a café-restaurant in the basement of the former. In the twenties that café was the meeting place of the St. Annes Chess Club.

Looking down North Crescent towards the Roman Catholic Church of Our Lady Star of the Sea, just in view on the left. This church was built as a memorial to the late Duchess of Norfolk and was mostly funded by the Duke, a friend of Squire Clifton of Lytham Hall and his brother Wykeham Clifton of Warton Hall.

The Imperial Hydropathic, surmounted by a statue erroneously believed by locals to be Britannia complete with trident was, fittingly for a hydro, Hygeia the Goddess of Health. Towards the end of the First World war the Hydro became a military hospital for officers. Restored to civilian use, it became the Majestic in 1923. In 1939 it became the headquarters of the Ministry of Food. The statue was removed, rumoured as an Air Raid precaution, and is believed to have been melted down for munitions.

or traipse their cattle across the town-field during the night. They might exchange hot words, and lift up their fists, and deal out a bloody nose or two ; and the goodwife might become involved in a brawl with her neighbour, or dandle her flax in a cattle pool, to the danger of the stock. But these were the unsubtle lapses of a simple people, and the more sophisticated crimes of the cities had no part in their lives.

Countrymen, yet they lived within sight of the sea, and they were static. The " sandgrown 'uns " had no ambitions to go out and conquer the world, but waited patiently for the world to come and discover them. And that it did from 1775 onwards. First in driblets, later in shoals, came the health-starved multitudes from an industrial county who were to take this backward little community by the scruff of the neck and shake it to vigorous life. " Foreigners ", they were, " off-comed-'uns ", but the silver jingling in their pockets was as music in sand-grown ears.

Lytham about 1830, showing Dicconson Terrace (centre), and the first Clifton Arms Hotel (background)—now Park Street. (*from a sketch by P. Whittle*)

Down came dilapidated cottages, and up went extensive hotels. The parish rang with new voices clamouring new needs. More fish and food, and meat and milk ; more bathing machines, and boats, and bowling greens, and brass bands ; good roads, and gas lamps, and coffee-houses, and cabs. These, and a hundred other facilities, were demanded by ever-increasing hordes of holiday-makers who had fallen in love with Lytham and taken it unto themselves.

By the middle of last century, the township of Lytham, as we know it, had emerged and begun to expand, and the folk of many counties had come here to stay. But at the further end of the parish, where one day another town would be born, there still lived the ancient " sand-grown 'uns " who remained almost untouched by modern events.

In tiny cots, in small isolated communities, they passed their existence amongst green fields and golden dunes, and with the boom of a mighty ocean ever in their ears. Always, they looked out to the westward and considered the weather, for they had lived for centuries within the menace of the uprising sea. They were a canny lot, and clannish, and they knew when and where to hold their tongues. But when they chose, they were great and fluent talkers, embellishing their tales with a wealth of dramatic gesture and inflection, and holding their fireside audiences spell-bound, often long into the night. Maybe it was caution, distrusting the present, that directed their conversations towards events of the past, and so the stories of old were handed down from father to son. Smugglers and wreckers they were, in the long, long ago, and there wasn't a native worth his salt who did not consider the Squire's rabbits and pheasants fair game.

The humour of the " sandgrown 'uns " was penetrating, often blunt, though softened, more often than not, by a comic turn of phrase or the disarming twinkle of an eye. If they liked the face of a stranger they would tell him (nearly) all, but let him arouse their suspicions, and in a flash they were uncommunicative, withdrawn.

They were a great people these salt-sprayed, weather-beaten " sandgrown 'uns." They might get in a cunning thrust or two at the expense of their neighbour, they would not hesitate to drive a hard bargain ; but they were hospitable and courageous, resilient and tough, and theirs was the inborn sagacity of men living close to the soil.

Never were their sterling qualities so clearly revealed as when they were called to the service of the lifeboat. Then without hesitation, these heroes who, from infancy, had known every caprice of our treacherous coast-water, went forth to the rescue of strangers, whilst their womenfolk from long practice had learned how to watch and wait.

These, then, were the old " sandgrown 'uns." Blue-jerseyed and bare-armed, and wearing the traditional peak-cap of their calling, they have largely disappeared from the scene. But this coastal strip of ours, the product of many invasions, human and non-human, of Romans, Angles, Norsemen, holiday makers and Lancashire business men, blowing sand, and the very sea itself, will yet bring forth many more generations who will be proud to be called " sand-grown."

LYTHAM

LYTHAM HALL, THE HOME OF THE CLIFTON FAMILY

Some time during the 17th century, an unknown artist pulled out the equivalent of an empty cigarette packet and began doodling amongst the sandhills of Lytham. The tattered fragment, now deposited with the County Records at Preston, gives us a fascinating glimpse of the old village, with its early Church of St. Cuthbert, a cluster of cottages, a peg and post wind-mill, and perhaps most exciting of all, the only sketch yet known to exist, of the first Lytham Hall.

(By courtesy of Mrs. Violet Clifton).

Lytham Hall, St. Cuthbert's Church and Lytham Township, from an undated fragment of manuscript in the Lancashire Record Office, Reference : DDCL/1056, probably early 17th century. (*Block kindly loaned by the Historic Society of Lancashire and Cheshire*).

Cuthbert Clifton, whose family's roots were struck deep into the Kirkham and Westby areas, soon after the Conquest, bought the manor of Lytham from Sir Richard Molyneux, in 1606. Immediately, he began pull.ng down the old priory and built in its place a gracious mansion with a distinctly Elizabethan flavour. It was probably completed by about 1610, and a few years later, in 1617, Cuthbert Clifton was knighted by James I at Lathom House.

Sir Cuthbert belonged to that typically English breed of farming gentry, and though " sickly in body," he left behind a robust family of 7 daughters

MAIN ENTRANCE GATE, LYTHAM HALL

Main entrance gates, Lytham Hall, from a design traditionally attributed to Sir Christopher Wren, and said to have been given by the architect to a former Squire of Lytham on the occasion of his marriage.
Block kindly loaned by the artist, Frank Dickinson, Esq., F.B.O.A. (Hons.)

and 5 sons whose descendants, since that time, have been tied in bonds of warmest affection with the people of Lytham.

Later, at some unknown date, Lytham Hall was at least partially destroyed by fire. In the middle of the 18th century Thomas Clifton, son of Thomas Clifton and the Hon. Mary Molyneux, commissioned the eminent architect, John Carr of York, to rebuild the Hall to its present gracious proportions. Carr's new creation, skilfully welded on to the remains of the old—the long gallery is the original, the servants' quarters, the chapel, and the enclosed courtyard where the Window Tax of 1696 prompted an economy of daylight and plunged the surrounding offices into almost cavernous gloom—produced what can now be regarded as possibly the most elegant Georgian house to be found in the whole of the county.

Lytham Hall, designed by Carr of York.(*Photograph by Alderman A. F. Williamson, C.C.*).

The ground floor salons are spacious and full of grace, and the eye is continually drawn to the fireplaces, each characteristic of the Adam period, and uniquely designed—and to the ceilings where the plasterwork varies from bold, though never oppressive, patterns to some of almost fairy-like delicacy. The withdrawing-room walls were hand-painted by 18th century Italian artists whose intricate designs, patiently executed, remind us forcefully of a more leisured age.

In the dining room, a magnificent semi-circular sideboard, an early Gillow piece carved from finest Honduras mahogany, especially for this setting, stands in a curved recess. It is not difficult to picture the elegant dinner parties which have been held in this gracious room which today, like all the others on the ground floor, is unfurnished. Once again, the superb moulding of the ceiling gives lightness and elegance to a room which relies solely on the Italian marble of the mantelpiece and the fascinating

16

Top left—Entrance Hall.   Bottom left—Dining Room.   Above—Staircase.

(Photographs by Saidman Brothers, Blackpool. Blocks by courteous arrangement with the Clifton Estate Office and the Rotary Club of Lytham).

collection of family portraits, for colour.

The staircase is impressively beautiful, perfectly balanced. From the first floor landing twin stairs spill down beneath a ceiling almost incredible in its magnificence. Here, in this powerful representation of the mighty Thor riding the heavens, is the faultless blending of craftsmanship and art.

On the first floor is a suite of rooms which Mrs. Violet Clifton, widow of our late Squire, has chosen for her own use. A large sunny room, overlooking the formal garden on the one side, and wide lawns, distant pastures, and majestic trees, on the other, has become the boudoir where Mrs. Clifton spends a great deal of her time. A portrait considered to be of Sir Cuthbert hangs on one of the walls, and in the window recess is a pleasing Lely study of Bridget, young daughter of Sir Thomas Clifton who was raised to the baronetcy in 1660 but who died without a male heir.

One always comes away from Lytham Hall with a kaleidoscopic impression of architectural splendours, and noble proportions ; of a host of family portraits recalling byegone days ; of the new skilfully " married " to the old (as in the billiards room which links up the original long gallery) ; of portraits of horses which one would expect from a family long connected with the turf ; of tasteful colour schemes chosen subtly to reflect the predominating theme of the paintings hanging in the apartments ; of crystal

17

chandeliers, of Russian and Oriental embroideries, of 17th century oak furniture, richly carved, and of items of chinoiserie which the present Squire, Mr. Harry de Vere Clifton, occasionally sends home.

There is a great deal of satisfaction locally, nowadays, in the thought that, at last, one of " the family " is back at the Hall. Since Mrs. Clifton, who is a gifted poet and writer, and whose " Book of Talbot " is one of the most poignant biographies ever written in the English language, returned to Lytham and became absorbed into the affairs and affections of its people, this traditional home of the Clifton family has been gradually restored to life and beauty, and use. Artists, scholars, and writers come calling once more, and there is always a special delight for those who are seeing the Hall for the first time.

The grounds themselves, as memorable as the house, leave a lasting impression of timelessness and tranquility ; of towering trees and expansive lawns, and pastures sprinkled with cattle ; of flocks of drab brown birds tramping about on the grass with all the blithe inconsequence of domestic poultry . . . until one realises, with a mild sense of shock, that these are pheasants ; of the gaudy flash of a cock bird diving under the laurels ; of high-banked rhododendrons, forbidding, or full of colour ; of an albino hare placidly lolloping across the meadow ; of a solitary roe-deer that came unbidden and made its home in the park ; of magnificent stables, endless carriage drives, and a towering dovecote which kept earlier generations supplied with fresh winter meat ; and of the imposing entrance gates which stood near the town centre until the coming of the railway, and of which the design has always been attributed to Sir Christopher Wren.

This, then, is the impressive home of an above-ordinary family, whose members have been sportsmen, travellers, writers, landlords, and farmers ; who have been linked in marriage with all the great families of the land ; who stood firm during the times of religious persecution ; and who, over a long period of time, have become part of Lytham itself.

THE PARISH CHURCH OF ST. CUTHBERT, LYTHAM

Within 200 yards of Lytham Parish Church, and nestling in a hedgerow, a stone cross bears a tablet inscribed as follows :—

" According to ancient tradition, the body of St. Cuthbert about the year 882 A.D. once rested here."

Earlier this century, and as a thank offering for recovery from severe illness, the late Canon Hawkins donated this modern cross. It was fixed into the old base socket which had stood at that point for as long as anyone in Lytham could remember. A large congregation, including several church dignatories, gathered at the roadside for the choral dedication ceremony performed by Archdeacon Hornby of Lancaster.

There are said to have been several thousands of these roadside crosses scattered about the highways of England before the Reformation, and there were several hundreds in Lancashire alone. They were set up largely in the centuries following the Conquest to remind our people that God was present in every walk of life, and was not just to be remembered on Sundays and in Church.

With the passage of time, many of these traditional wayside shrines were either plundered, defaced, or altogether removed, but the one restored to Lytham lives on in perpetual memory of her patron saint.

The solitary shepherd lad first saw a vision on the hills of Lammermuir and rose to become one of the greatest Christian missionaries of all time. He pushed his lonely way through the wildest parts of the country, and his death in 686 on desolate Farne Island gave rise to all manner of mystical legends which spread like ripples on a pool and drew many pilgrims to his shrine.

Years after his death, they looked into his tomb, and we are told . . . "whiles they opened his coffin they start at a wonder, they lookt for bones and found flesh, they expected a skeleton and saw an entire body with joynts flexible, his flesh so succulent that there only wanted heate . . . nay, his very funeral weeds were as fresh as if putrefaction had not dared to take him by the coat."

So the years passed, and the Danes attacked Lindisfarne. The monks snatched up the saint's remains and fled, portering their sacred burden throughout the north, and for long harassed years. Where the body had rested, crosses were often set up in memory of the saint whose relics were finally brought to Durham in the closing years of the 10th century. If, years later, a church was built alongside such a cross, it was natural that it should be dedicated to St. Cuthbert.

Lytham's connection with the saint, then, had already been established when Richard Fitz Roger bequeathed Lytham to the monks of Durham for the setting up of a Benedictine Priory here in 1190. (Actually, Lytham, like Penwortham, was really a cell, to which monks were sent for shortish periods to overlook the mother priory's possessions in the area). Though the Domesday Survey made no reference to a church in Lytham, it is now almost beyond doubt that one, possibly of Celtic origins, had functioned for many years before.

In Reginald of Durham's records it was noted that Richard's grandfather, Ravenkill, had seen a sparrow alighting on the altar of a ruined wooden church, and had demolished it and caused it to be rebuilt in stone on a neighbouring site. Besides the church, there was also an old burial ground mentioned, though whether this referred to Kilgrimol, or to some other portion of the coast now overwashed by the sea, it is difficult to establish.

At any rate, Ravenkill's new stone (probably shingle) church was set up near the present site, and dedicated to St. Cuthbert. It was a low and humble building, though commodious enough for the tiny population who referred to it as " the cathedral." It had old oak pews, a pulpit against the south wall, and a crooked porch. To this little cobble church, in solemn file and with their cowls pulled about their ears, the three monks (there were never more than this number, though included amongst the secular appointments were a parish priest, a senechal, a clerk, two or more pages, and several domestic and farm servants, etc.) would come in silent procession from the Priory.

By 1760, this ancient structure, parts at least of which were the original, had fallen into such a grievous state of disrepair as to constitute a distinct danger to all who dared sit, quaking fearfully, beneath its sagging roof.

Lytham had not yet benefited by the arrival of the sea-bathers, and " the parish being very small and petitioners mostly tenants at rack rents and burdened with numerous poor," it became urgently necessary to launch a nationwide appeal for funds to restore " the said church of Lytham." In the Church Brief of 1763, authorising " the Minister and churchwardens to go from house to house," and to seek contributions from " Ministers, curates and preachers and persons called Quakers," the crumbling church was described as :

> ". . . a very ancient structure standing upon the sea coast and so much decayed in every part that the parishioners cannot assemble therein for the worship of God without manifest danger of their lives, the walls being so bulged out in some places near three feet from the perpendicular, that the parishioners have laid out considerable sums of money from time to time in repairing and endeavouring to support the said church, yet the same is by length of time become so ruinous and decayed that it cannot any longer be kept up, but the same with the steeple must be taken down and rebuilt."

The estimate for rebuilding, exclusive of all old materials, was £1,373 17s. 8d., which sum was obtained, allowing the demolition and rebuilding to be put in hand. Fortunately, our 17th century artist captured for all time the only sketch in existence of the original St. Cuthbert's Church. (see page 13)

The second St. Cuthbert's Church, from an old water colour.

The new church, sturdily built, with walls above a yard in thickness, was no more imposing than its predecessor. It incorporated the east and west walls of the original church, and showed little originality or vision. The interior was plain, though elegant, with narrow oak forms, a pulpit on the south, and tablets to the memory of members of the Clifton family whose remains, through long generations, had lain at St. Cuthbert's.

The church was whitewashed, and its tower steeple at the western end ensured an admirable landmark for Ribble shipping.

Strangely enough, the first church served the community for the best part of 600 years, but its successor, within sixty years, was to be pulled down. Obviously the Lythamers had had no indication of the sea-bathing influx which, within a few years, was to take the township by storm. Else they

20

would have been more ambitious with their church re-building project and would have looked far beyond their own limited needs.

As it was, the church, especially in the summer months, was crowded to overflowing with visitors who were completely undeterred by the long dusty trudge over Hungry Moor (now Lowther Gardens). By the 1830's, Lytham had learned in some measure how to cater for her fashionable crowds. Hotels which had been swiftly rushed up were as speedily pulled down where they were found to interfere with the over-all development of the resort. Now, without hesitation, the new whitewashed Church of St. Cuthbert was set aside, and the present one was built and opened for divine service before the end of 1834.

It is a lovely church and well worth a visit for the beauty and dignity of the interior and for the added interest of its having been built for the sea-bathers, many of whom fell in love with Lytham, came here to stay, and laid their bones to rest amongst the " sandgrown 'uns."

The present Church, built 1834. (*Block by courtesy of " Lytham Standard " Printing Co. Ltd.*)

GETTING HERE IN THE FIRST PLACE !

That anyone, during the 18th century, managed to arrive in Lytham from The Great World Beyond speaks highly for human endurance and determination.

Despite the Highways Act of 1555, which had firmly placed the responsibility for maintaining roads and bridges on the shoulders of each parish, and obliged all householders to turn out, first for four, and later for six, days in each year to put their roads in good order, the highways of Lancashire remained stubbornly and notoriously bad.

" Twelve miles of such ground as I never rode in all my life," declared Oliver Cromwell of one of them, whilst 17th century poet Richard James bewailed them collectively in these terms :

" Our wayes are gulphs of durt and mire which none
Scarce ever passe in summer without moane."

What then, prompts imagination, must it have been like in the winter ?

From 1663 Acts of Parliament authorised the construction of turnpike roads by which passage was effected on payment of tolls. Not unnaturally, industrial areas, relying on all-year-round transport of raw materials and coals, were the first to develop new road systems by this method, and by 1790 two thousand Acts had been passed and there was a network of turnpike roads strung over the English countryside.

Travelling by coach, however, which had been rendered safer, pleasanter and quicker, was still not without its perils. Footpads lurked in hiding, so that for greater safety travellers arranged to move about in groups. The accident rate was considerable, breakdowns were frequent, and boisterous winds, slippery roads, or swollen fords could, and did, cause intolerable delays.

Read what Arthur Young wrote in an angry moment in 1770 after negotiating the road between Preston and Wigan :

" To look over a map and perceive that the road is a principal one, not merely between towns, but also a highway between high counties, one would naturally conclude it to be at least decent, but let me seriously caution all travellers who may by chance purpose to travel this terrible country to avoid it as they would the devil, for a thousand to one they break their necks or their limbs by overthrows or breakings down. They will here meet with ruts which I actually measured four feet deep and floating with mud . . . The only mending it receives is the tumbling in of loose stones, which serve no other purpose but to jolt a carriage in the most intolerable manner. These are not merely opinions, but facts, for I actually passed three carts broken down in these eighteen miles of most wretched memory."

If industrial Lancashire fared thus badly, we can reckon that the Fylde folk fared rather worse. From Preston to Kirkham they took their choice between the King's highway which was " very ruinous and in bad repair and of an unnecessary length " and the " private way over Lea and Clifton Marshes " which was " frequently overflowed by the tides . . . and sometimes impassable."

In 1718 Sir Thomas Clifton and Sir Henry Hoghton, neighbouring local landowners, laid plans to construct a short stretch of stone-paved road, to by used on payment of tolls, and to be all of twelve feet wide ! Along this miserable highway, standing like a perilous platform between two capacious ditches floating with mud, the first intrepid visitors were to make their way to the coast.

From Kirkham onwards any pretence at road-making dwindled away altogether, and the first sea-bathers were faced with a tangle of rutted tracks which came from nowhere and led in the same direction. With no Black-

The Pier, Lytham.

2609.   7.

Lytham Pier in its hey-day, featuring one of the entrance kiosks and the cinema. It must be an early photograph, taken before the Floral Hall at the far end and the adjacent jetty had been added. Regular steamer services to Southport, Llandudno, Fleetwood and Barrow by the Lytham Shipping Company were a feature of a visit to Lytham in those days.

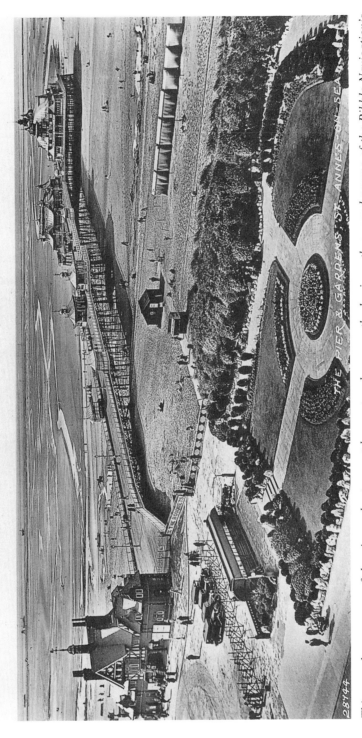

THE PIER & GARDENS, ST. ANNES-ON-SEA.

This superb panorama of the pier and estuary at low water shows, on the horizon, three sand pumps of the Ribble Navigation's dredging fleet. They maintained the channel at a sufficient depth for the ships visiting the Port of Preston. The photo is taken from the roof of the Majestic Hotel, from where the best view of the pier and beach could be had.

pool Tower to serve as a landmark, they frequently meandered ineffectually and protractedly around outlying fields before arriving, saddle-sore or foot-weary, in Lytham. Except for a chance lift in a carrier's cart, or having the means to maintain a private carriage, all the first visitors came by foot or on horseback. It was not until about 1771 that even the important town of Preston had its first stage-coach.

We can picture the nicely-placed visitor trotting along the private toll road with his bouncy wife perched up behind on the sociable pillion, whilst the less fortunate trudged the same route with bag and baggage.

It must have been a memorable day for Lytham when the first stage coach service was established, and the rattling vehicle, with many a smart crack of the whip, many a full-throated blast from the horn, and with cries from an overflowing cargo of excited visitors, swept with a flourish into the market square after completing the journey at a spanking nine miles per hour.

Doors would spill open and the whole populace would tear out, to greet the wheeled messenger from The Great World Outside, to ply the coachman with curious questions, and to stare with amazement at the most wondrous spectacle of the age.

During the 1820's, however, the road came under spirited fire from irritated travellers. " There is a road leading from Kirkham than which I do not know a worse, or a more dangerous," growled one. " The present road is one merely of sufferance, and the traveller is perpetually in danger of being soused in a ditch," grumbled another. Obviously this private toll road which ought to have proved a boon had, with the increased traffic, become a bane.

The delirious joy which heralded the railway's coming to Lytham can not only be imagined, but indeed was reflected in the colourful scenes of celebration which attended the event.

THE RAILWAY IS BROUGHT TO LYTHAM

On the 15th July, 1840, the Preston and Wyre Railway, linking the new dock town of Fleetwood with the rest of the world, was formally opened, thanks to the unwearied efforts of Sir Peter Hesketh Fleetwood, Bart., of Rossall Hall (M.P. for Preston), the interest and approbation of most of the eminent engineers in the kingdom, and funds amounting to £260,000 which the $19\frac{1}{2}$ miles had cost.

Well-wishers from all parts converged upon Fleetwood to enjoy a meal sent down by the Castle Inn of Preston, and the Bull Inn at Poulton. Lytham, meantime, made shift to smother her envy, and prepared to wait another six years to be linked up by rail.

At last the day came. On 16th February, 1846, the flags went up in Lytham, and the " sandgrown 'uns " took another day off to celebrate the arrival of the railway. A branch line, less than five miles in length and stemming from the main line at a point approximately a mile north-west of Kirkham, had brought our ancient township into close and convenient touch with the world.

An illustrious company of directors, well-known public figures and neighbouring gentry, foregathered at Lytham Hall for a commemorative luncheon. Within the town, meantime, banners and bunting fluttered, brass bands marched, and happy crowds swarmed in the streets and choked the station approach.

To excited cheers and the thunderous discharge of cannon, The Squire and Mrs. Clifton (the only lady in the party), along with their guests, boarded the decorated train which chugged away with smuts descending upon the 14 open carriages. The return journey is said to have been completed in 15 minutes !

The first station—opened in 1846. (*Photograph by Alderman A. F. Williamson, C.C.*)

Far into the February evening the jollifications continued within the taverns of Lytham, and no-one could be blamed for stealing back to take another look at the station building, with its neat stonework, its balustrade, and noble columns. It was a building to be proud of from the outside, and to inspire admiration from within. The central octagonal booking hall rose up in lofty splendour. Waiting rooms provided accommodation for all classes of travellers, and gave directly on to a platform behind the buffers. Another platform ran along the outside wall, and above the whole spread a roof 140 feet long and 53 feet wide, supported by twelve massive wooden arches made up of segments screwed and bolted together.

Three small cottages were provided by the Company at the rear for use by the station master, engine driver and fireman, and from the first day onwards, no advertising matter was allowed to spoil the elevation.

Needless to say, when cheap Sunday trips to Preston were first introduced, not everybody was in favour of the general populace careering about the countryside at cut rates. Such a practice, it was feared, would rapidly undermine attendances at church, and protests to that effect were registered with the Company. Their Secretary, in 1846, assured certain gentlemen that . . . " If the evils you anticipate are realised by the experiment of cheap trains, the subject shall again receive the serious attention of the Board with an earnest desire to remove the cause of complaint ! "

No-one, however, could halt the trend towards travel for all, and in 1863 Mr. Clifton opened a single line, seven-and-a-half miles length of track linking Lytham and Blackpool. Again it was a joyous occasion for the increasingly travel-minded " sandgrown 'uns " and church bells and bunting celebrated this long-needed facility. Eight years later the line was amalgamated with the Preston and Wyre Company, and in 1874 the track was doubled and connected with the Kirkham—Lytham line.

The late Mr. John Townsend, who was born in 1851, and tipped the second load of bricks at St. Anne's Church site, remembered the first railway engine running between Lytham and Blackpool. Intending passengers from the West End of the parish used to run across the fields and wave their hands, hoping that the driver of the little green train would see them and pull to a halt at Gillett's Crossing. When the new Lytham station was built, the engine, called " Little Queen " was removed from one station to the other. It was dragged by seventeen horses across the fields which became Westby Street, and John Townsend's father took two horses along to join the team. It was a laborious business, but eventually the engine arrived safely at its destination after having been hauled a few yards at a time over a pathway of railway sleepers.

From that point, Lytham's original handsome old station discontinued its passenger service and, except for a few " special " excursions, was relegated to parcels and goods. A year or two ago even that service came to an end. Doors were locked which had seen the comings and goings of Victorian travellers. The laughter and bustle were stilled when the new station took over, and nowadays one is sad to see the old one quietly dying behind a brave front.

As a matter of general historical interest, it should be pointed out here that every resort on the Lancashire coast dates its rapid growth from the arrival of the railroad. Southport, Lytham and Morecambe were all being linked up about the same time ; (Morecambe 1848 ; Southport 1848-50).

LYTHAM DOCKS AND THE CUSTOM HOUSE

Nowadays it is difficult to believe that Lytham once enjoyed wide repute as a port. But take a walk seawards along the footpath beside the stone bridge on the main road leaving Lytham, and you will see the remains of rotting wooden wharves poking out from vast banks of accumulated silt. It is a spectacle washed over with the grey of desolation and decay and yet, in 1825, Lytham's mud dock was described as being " large enough to contain a fleet of men of war."

During long industrial years, large vessels put in at this natural harbour and discharged their cargoes into small lighters to be taken to Preston, whilst the merchants of that town were energetically squabbling and denouncing the Ribble Company's utter failure to provide them with adequate navigational facilities.

If, around 1830, and during those bitter Prestonian wrangles, Squire Clifton had chosen to invest in substantial wharves and docks, Preston Dock might never have come into being. At the Lancaster Assizes of 1824 he had established his claim " for anchorage on vessels loading and unloading there," and the temperamental Ribble, providing good deep channels for Lytham, and withholding them from Preston, would have ensured a sound commercial proposition for the local landowner.

Fortunately, for those who love the restful charm of Lytham, he declined to become involved in a venture which might have ensured financial return,

Lytham Mud Dock showing remains of wooden wharves and sluice gates. (*Photograph by Alderman A. F. Williamson, C.C.*).

but which would undoubtedly have attracted ugliness and the less desirable accompaniments of dockland activity to a strip of unspoiled coast.

It was not until 1840 that Mr. Clifton agreed to the construction of wharves and a dock at Lytham Pool. By this time the second Ribble Navigation Company had sprung into being whose proprietors had faith in bringing sufficient tidal waters to Preston by a policy of dredging and the building of training walls.

Whilst they got on with their schemes, however, Lytham enjoyed all the fuss and clatter of mercantile activity. A branch line of the railway was brought across the fields, over the road, and ran directly on to the wharves. Cranes hoisted the merchandise from ships lying snugly on the soft sandy bottom of the dock and conveniently lowered it into wagons to be taken by rail to Preston and beyond.

Not only Lytham-bound cargo ships made their way into the pool. Passing vessels encountering sudden squalls in the Ribble would frequently make for the sheltered harbour of Lytham and tie up there until the weather mended its ways.

Against this background of mercantile and marine activity, we can set the tree-flanked square little tower standing at the end of Lytham Beach. This brick and shingle Custom House, which always piques the curiosity of the visitor, was in no way connected with H.M. Customs and Excise.

It was built around 1850 to provide a look-out for Ribble shipping, possibly to discourage smuggling, and certainly to collect the Squire's harbour dues from vessels lying at anchor.

From the Clifton Cash Book of 1865 we discover that Captain Robert Whalley had collected two months' dock dues, amounting to £39 16s. 8d., for which his allowance was £4 3s. 4d. For his salary of £25 per annum (though in 1816 his predecessor, Thomas Cookson, had received only Ten Guineas!), he was obliged to row out, or walk out, to collect his employer's fees.

Arrivals and departures were reported to the Preston Custom House until 1879. By that time Preston Dock's importance had increased in proportion to Lytham's decline. Whether by reason of the training walls, or from natural forces, the capricious Ribble had shifted her course so that by 1884 her main channel ran a mile distant from Lytham Dock. And by that time the vigorous Prestonians had ambitious plans afoot for a dock and tidal basin.

Lytham shipping fell off to such an extent that the branch railway was put out of action, and from 1885 Lytham Dock, silted up and looking extremely sorry for itself, virtually ceased to function.

The Liggard Brook bringing drainage water in from low-lying lands still comes in at Graving Dock Bridge. The weight of tidal waters closes the sluice gates beneath the parapet by the roadside, and at low water the gates are pushed open as the Liggard discharges into the creek.

Lytham has had long connections with the sea and the building of boats, and you can still hear the clang and crash of the boatbuilders and repairers at work. Small vessels and sailing craft come up the creek at high tide to be tied up on the banks awaiting attention. The ebbing tide leaves them high and dry in a graving dock provided by nature, and you can spot them from the road, clusters of motor vessels and small yachts, waiting for week-end when their owners will take them out on the tide. Beyond, you can still see the large buildings left over from the days when Lytham Dockyard supplied paddle steamers, ferry boats and the like, for the waterways of the world.

But what of the Custom House? Did it die, along with the dock? Fortunately it entered into the second phase of its life when its solitary setting and ample lighting appealed to the talented local artist, Hugh B. Scott, whose river scenes, produced in this small tower studio, made his name. He was a beauty lover in every sense of the word. For thirty years he reclaimed the soil buried several feet beneath the shingle on which the tower was built. Austrian pines and rose trees, poplars and privet, vegetables and all manner of flowers, brought new beauty and usefulness to this half-acre plot.

After Hugh Scott's death early in the last war, the sturdy little tower served as the Headquarters of the Naval Cadets, but in recent years neglect and vandalism have bitten sorely into its walls. Now, development projects have decreed that one of these days it will come down, and another fragment of Lytham's history will have vanished from the scene.

BATH STREET, LYTHAM

In this quiet little street near to the centre of Lytham there are some interesting cottages, and fine samples of an almost forgotten local craft in the cobble pavements dated 1848.

They were experts, these men, who, with infinite care, selected pebbles smoothed and rounded by the tides of centuries and set them tightly interlocked to endure for ever. Boys served their time to this trade and acquired the skills of their masters. Cement was rarely used, but a quick eye and a cunning hand had ensured that the cobbles, once rammed home, were beyond the mischief of man to dislodge. Around the local farms travelled the craftsmen and their apprentices, selecting and pounding until they had produced a cobble yard tough enough to withstand the trampling of hooves and the passage of iron rimmed wheels, and durable enough to last for generations.

The Bath Street pavements which, but for Mrs. Clifton's intervention a few months ago, might have been asphalted over, show the old craft applied to work of a finer grade, and even after 112 years these story-soaked cobbles look like out-lasting any modern paving materials.

Bath Street became so named because, in the early days of Lytham's fame, it crossed the Green and gave onto that portion of the beach reserved for strictly segregated sea-bathing. The ladies were ushered from the vicinity when the gentlemen were bathing. Similarly, at least in theory,

Cobble pavement, Bath Street. (*Photograph by Alderman A. F. Williamson, C.C.*).

the heavily clad lady bathers could step from their striped machines untroubled by Peeping Toms. Clanging bells announced the changeover of the sexes. In these bikini-strewn days this may seem like a quaint and humorous over emphasis on personal modesty but, if accounts are to be believed, it would appear that often the lusty 19th century bather tossed discretion and clothing to the four winds and raced to meet the oncoming tide wearing only a smile on his face. Scenes of impropriety were a daily occurrence during the summer season, to the considerable entertainment of passers-by. A House of Correction was only established in Lytham after the arrival of the sea-bathers. It provided accommodation for both sexes, and it stood in Douglas Street which has disappeared now, but which at one time might have formed part of Clifton Street.

How Lytham reacted to the high-jinks of the visitors is reflected in a resolution by the Commissioners, in the early years of the Improvement Act (passed in 1847). Henceforth, the local constable was to be paid 1s. 0d. each Sunday to supervise the bathing, to discourage horse-play and immodesty, and to " enforce the regulations " to the letter. The Commissioners were determined upon dealing severely with any infringement of the rules.

Quite apart from its marine connections, Bath Street has other significance. One of the cottages was a licensed preaching house in the early years of last century. There lived Mr. Mercer, long generations of whose family lie sleeping in St. Cuthbert's churchyard, and whose descendents still dwell in Lytham. At that time Wesleyan Methodism had gained no foothold in this parish which, apart from a small Baptist nucleus, was sharply divided between the Established Church and the teachings of Rome.

From the 1780's, when Lytham was attracting her first visitors, young Methodist converts from Preston were blazing a fruitless trail through the villages and hamlets of the Fylde. Harsh words and hostility were their portion, with physical violence and onslaughts from village bulldogs thrown in for good measure. Geographical isolation had rendered the Fylde folk unreceptive, rigid, and highly resistant to new ideas, and the clannish natives would have no truck with the new fangled preaching.

By contrast, in Pilling, of all remote places, and entirely due to the zeal of one local convert, Methodism got off to a flying start in 1811. In that same year Moses Holden of Kirkham and Preston was doggedly plodding in the footsteps of his forerunners, but the entries in his journal show that Methodism, even after 30 years, had made poor progress in the Fylde. Poulton, which had rudely man-handled the first evangelists thirty years earlier, now boasted ten members, and to rally these, and any other new converts along the Fylde coastal strip, Moses Holden set out from Preston in the January of 1811.

After preaching at Thornton and Marton, he arrived at Lytham and made straight for Mr. Mercer's house in Bath Street where formerly a Mr. Lyon had held a licence to preach, though by now it had been given up. Holden determined to open the house again, and thereby drew both good congregations and an acrimonious broadside from the local Vicar.

By Holden's telling, the Vicar arrived at the house, kicked up a commotion, and demanded to have sight of the licence. When Mercer's daughter produced the offending document he snorted and puffed and threatened to put a stop to their activities. She in turn retorted that the licence was valid for as long as one stone stood upon another, and the Vicar stormed off to enlist the Squire's help in prohibiting Methodism and banishing Holden from Lytham. With characteristic independence of mind, however, The Squire not only refused to oblige, but also threatened to instal Holden in the Vicar's place if the persecutions continued. " He troubled us no more after that," ran Holden's comment.

During the following year, Moses Holden had managed to form classes in several neighbouring villages, but he was obliged to record of this parish : " I never could prevail on the Lytham people to join the Society. They received me kindly, and heard me gladly, but that was all . . ."

Rigidity and apathy defeated all the preacher's efforts to sow the seeds of Methodism in Lytham. But the Wesleyan movement had not yet finished with Bath Street where, more than thirty years later, a courageous woman and her husband were to inspire the building of the first Wesleyan Chapel.

THE WESLEYAN CHAPEL IN BATH STREET

No doubt the Vicar of Lytham breathed a sigh of relief when Preacher Holden trudged out of the parish. But in Cobridge, Staffordshire, at that time, a little girl was growing up who would one day help to establish the teachings of Wesley in the North-West.

Her name was Dorothy, and she was born in 1802. Her father was a master potter, her mother an intelligent and strong-minded woman who believed in spiritual freedom for her children.

At a tender age, Dorothy was stolen by the gypsies. She was rescued by a posse of neighbours who hoisted her from a hamper on one of the carts. The child was calmly munching gingerbread at the time and her rescuers were vastly impressed with this unruffled behaviour. Whatever the colourful predictions for her future on that account, however, they fell far short of events as they were to unfold.

During Dorothy's adolescence, her dying mother extracted a faithful promise from the father that the children's spiritual freedom would be preserved. But a year or two later, when Dorothy accompanied a friend to Burslem to hear a Wesleyan preacher and came home fired with Methodist ideas, the sacred promise was speedily retracted. Relations between father and daughter became progressively strained and were finally severed when Dorothy refused to renounce her devotion to the Methodist cause.

" Give it up or never darken my doors again " seems to have been the operative phrase as Dorothy left the old family home, went into cheap lodgings and tried to keep body and soul together by painting china. Poorly paid she must have been, and under-nourished she certainly was. Eventually her health gave way, her father relented, and the servants were despatched to carry the erring daughter home. Not even a tender reconciliation could deflect Dorothy's determination, however, and her work for Methodism continued unabated.

At the age of 22 she even went so far as to marry one of the " detested new preachers," and their honeymoon was spent aboard a sailing vessel, surrounded by all their worldly belongings, bound for a life of mission work in the West Indies. They landed in Antigua in 1825 and life seemed good and full of promise to the young Mr. and Mrs. Jones.

Indeed, nothing seemed amiss twelve months later as the young pair, along with five other missionaries and their wives and children, boarded the mail steamer " Maria " after a district meeting on a neighbouring island and set off happily for home.

But these were treacherous waters. Storms could blow up in an instant, and one now hurled itself with tropical harshness upon the doomed "Maria" when she was all too close to a sinister reef. With bitter irony, land was in sight as the vessel cast up on her beam ends, lost her lifeboats in the swell, and tossed most of her company instantly to the sharks. But for a tangle of ropes Dorothy too would have shared that horrifying fate. The captain lashed her more firmly before he joined the victims, and the handful of survivors, including Mr. Jones, who had managed to cling on for dear life, each in turn succumbed to exhaustion and exposure until only Dorothy, badly injured by shattered timbers, remained alive.

Four days later two fishermen, idly skulling past the wreck, noticed a grotesque black scarecrow swaying rope-lashed to the bowsprit. This was what was left of a woman, after four nights of thirst and hunger, four days of the merciless sun, and never-ending hours of unspeakable horror. They rowed her the three miles back to land, and there she was slowly nursed back to convalescence. Now it was her destiny to leave the mission field, with all its harsh memories, and return to the home of her father in England, and to her Methodist work.

Six years later she married Mr. Thomas Crouch Hincksman of Preston, another great Methodist worker. They toiled together for many years in Preston's dockland, carrying their message into the slums, setting up Sunday Schools for ragged children, mending broken homes, and infusing new hope into this dismal resort of rowdies and roughnecks.

At the age of 45, however, Dorothy Hincksman's health sharply declined. Her sickness was diagnosed as advanced tuberculosis of the lungs, and, very near to death, she was brought to Lytham where, with her family, she had spent many happy holiday hours. Miraculously, the fine pure air of our coast restored her strength at a time when the church authorities at Preston were beginning to think in terms of establishing a Wesleyan Chapel in Lytham. The Hincksman's were living at No. 5 Dicconson Terrace, which, it is thought in certain quarters, was the first slated house in Lytham. They and their friends began looking about for a suitable site, and by strange coincidence, the one most favoured happened to be almost opposite the old licensed preaching house in Bath Street where the Vicar had come blustering and Moses Holden had laboured in vain.

Once again, the intrusion of Methodism did not go unnoticed at the Vicarage, and in a sharp letter to the Clifton Agent, the incumbent was moved to protest :

> " Having heard that you, with four strangers, yesterday fixed on a site for the erection of a chapel (?) for the encouragement of schism and the propogation of dissent, I feel it necessary, as the only author-ised spiritual pastor according to Christ's ordinance and the laws of this country, to protest against this invasion of my parish " . . . (which step he was convinced, could only create) . . . " division, anger, animosity, suspicion, and a sort of exclusive dealing induced by this new and permanent position in which dissent will be placed."

These protests fell on deaf ears. A 99-year lease was granted to William Humber and permission was granted for the building of a Wesleyan Chapel which would accommodate 200 worshippers. Meantime, the movement had so vigorously taken root that within a score of years the building proved quite inadequate to seat all its members, and in 1868 the much larger Park Street Methodist Church premises were built.

From that point the Bath Street Chapel ceased to function, as such, but it is interesting to recall that, during its lifetime, in 1857 to be exact, the Squire of Lytham, Mr. John Talbot Clifton, who owned the Neptune (now Queen's) Hotel, gave an assurance to the Chapel Trustees " that no windows " (in the recently added billiards room, later the dining room at the hotel) . . . " will be facing on the chapel yard." That promise was upheld long after the chapel had closed, and even up to very recent years.

From 1868 the building served a variety of purposes. First it was a coffee house, then a reading room and literary institute, and later it was purchased by the Lodge of Triumph for £300 and became known as The Masonic Hall. After that, for twenty years, it served as a furniture saleroom where auctions were held in the shadow of the old choir stalls and gallery.

During the second world war there arrived American troops whose breezy exuberance swept aside all the cobwebs from the past. Highly coloured murals depicting ape-like figures kept some unknown G.I. with a

Wesleyan Chapel, Bath Street, built 1846. (*Photograph by Alderman A. F. Williamson, C.C.*).

precocious talent hard at work transforming the solemn old walls into a more acceptable setting for a " Dough-Nut Dug-Out."

In 1945 the property passed into the hands of the Lytham-St. Annes Corporation from whom it was eventually acquired by the Lancashire County Council. Now, perhaps finally, its destiny had been settled. Lytham's first Wesleyan Chapel was to become a Clinic, and Tom Mellor, Lytham's own brilliant young architect (whose restoration of the Market House, Lytham, is worthy of the highest praise), supervised the conversion of the interior for use by this important health service.

As a tailpiece to the story, Mrs. Dorothy Hincksman was spared for twelve years of work at Lytham, and died, aged 57, in 1859. Her husband, who was a grand old gentleman of Methodism and greatly beloved in this district, continued his work into great age and left behind a prospering church when he died in 1883.

Their son, Major Wm. Henry Hincksman, a cotton manufacturer at Preston, took over " The Starr Hills," former home of Richard Ansdell, R.A., whose studies of wind-blown dogs, wind-tossed sheep, and wind-swept animals of all kinds, made him famous, and after whom the locality was named.

Major Hincksman's wife, Louisa, was herself the daughter of a missionary Samuel Broadbent, and in June 1958, when " The Starr Hills " was opened as a Methodist Home for the Aged, their grand-daughter, Dr. Dorothy Hincksman Farrar, Vice-President of the Methodist Conference in 1952, performed the dedication ceremony.

Thus this powerful story of Methodist pioneering came full circle, with the past commemorated in a bronze plaque in one of the rooms at " The Starr Hills," and on a tablet in the Park Street Methodist Church, Lytham. The final words read :

" They rest from their labours and their works do follow them."

ST. PETER'S ROMAN CATHOLIC CHURCH,

It has been said that during the times of severe persecutions of Roman Catholics in the 16th and 17th centuries, Lancashire put forward more young men to be trained for the priesthood than any other county in England, and that the Fylde provided more candidates than the whole of Lancashire.

St. Peter's R.C. Church, Lytham. (*Block kindly loaned by "Lytham Standard" Printing Co. Ltd.*)

This must be some measure of the tenacity of the north-westerners who, taking their lead from the landed families, kept the flame of Roman Catholicism burning defiantly, if secretly, in these parts.

Cardinal Allen, a native of Rossall, a little way along the coast, arch-enemy and sharp thorn in the flesh of the first Queen Elizabeth, had incurred the Sovereign's undying displeasure by founding a college for the training of Roman Catholic priests at Douai, on the Continent. Sons of well-to-do families were secretly shipped across the Channel, evading the keen eyes of Elizabeth's agents and returning a few years later to continue under-cover activities for the faith.

Plots, priestholes, narrow escapes, rumours, and sudden swift swoops by Government spies, were all woven into the tapestry of Fylde history, and a stranger upon the road was enough to flush out the quarry from his devotions and either send him scurrying over the fields to take refuge in cottage or hall, or prompt him to reach for his smock and busy himself about the milk pails in the cowshed, since, very often the priest was disguised as a household servant. Scarcely an important family in this area swerved in its loyalty to Rome, and though many of them put in a nominal attendance at their parish church, it was only to return home later to their secret devotions.

Geographically remote, the Fylde escaped much of the heavy-handed persecution meted out in more accessible districts. Hoodwinking the authorities, Jesuit priests moved slickly and with, at least, comparative impunity about the community. And on Sundays and Holy Days, the devout of this area straggled over the fields to their devotions in the private chapel of Westby Hall.

Lytham Hall, of course, was ever the scene of Roman Catholic activities. Along with a goodly proportion of the adult population who stubbornly refused to acknowledge the Sovereign as head of the church in England, the Squire and his lady were duly registered as recusants. Confiscation marched hand in hand with these Romish addictions, but the Clifton family continued to maintain a priest and private chapel at the Hall, and to afford facilities for worship to the inhabitants.

Around the year 1800, when the penal days were almost over and Roman Catholic services had been tolerated by the law for a century, a tithe barn which has now disappeared (no-one seems to know where), was allocated to the Lytham Catholics for their devotions. The priest lived at the house called " Woodlands," at Ansdell, from where he is said to have called the faithful by tolling a bell.

In 1839 St. Peter's Roman Catholic Church was built at Lytham, with accommodation for 700 worshippers. The Catholic School premises were acquired in 1850, and a house was taken over as a presbytery.

There have been many additions since to both Church and School, including an infants' department in 1874, new sacristies and side chapels in 1875, and a High Altar, Lady Altar and St. Joseph's Altar in 1877.

In the following year, Colonel John Talbot Clifton, Roman Catholic husband of Protestant Lady Eleanor Cecily, raised the great tower. There were new benches in 1893, a peal of six bells and stained glass windows in 1894, new altars and an enlarged sanctuary in 1897, and the lych gate in 1899. A burial ground and chapel were acquired about the same time.

Whatever the fluctuations of the past, Roman Catholicism is now established on a deep-rooted and solid basis along the Fylde coast of Lancashire, and in addition to St. Peter's, there are fine churches of that persuasion in both Ansdell and St. Annes.

The white-bearded gentleman, bowing to the applause following his speech on the occasion of his crowning the Lytham Rose Queen in front of the old Lytham Baths building, is Augustus Wykeham Clifton, brother of Squire John Talbot Clifton who is sitting with his wife to the left of the picture which was taken in the early years of the century.

St. Annes Pier about the turn of the century; the picture is taken from the Southdown Hydro which, in 1926, became the Town Hall for the Borough of Lytham St. Annes. This hotel was just across the road from the Hotel Majestic which was originally the 200-roomed Imperial Hydro.

The promenaders on St. Annes Pier are dated, not by their dresses, but by the Imperial Hydro on the left and the Southdown Hydro on the right. The right-hand section of the Imperial opened on Christmas day, 1910; the second half was finished in 1917, so the picture was taken between after then.

THE MARKET HOUSE AT LYTHAM

Sea-bathing alone put Lytham on the map. During the 18th century English seamen and travellers had seen the South Sea Islanders disporting themselves in the water with enjoyment and apparent impunity. The revolutionary idea of immersing the human body gradually caught on in this country. Caution still reigned in some quarters, but when George III took up the craze and developed a fondness for Weymouth, fashionable society slavishly followed suit. Well-to-do holiday makers descended upon hitherto undiscovered seaside communities wherever bathing facilities existed, and hard upon their heels came the less well-off whose long hours in mill and factory had blanched their cheeks and sent them scuttling coastwards for restoration.

Lytham, Blackpool and Southport, were the natural choice for the industrial multitudes from the Lancashire hinterlands. The first visitors, undeterred by lack of travel facilities, atrocious roads, and the poverty-stricken appearance of the hamlet, began to straggle into Lytham during the 1770's. Presently, whether by cart, on horseback, or as likely on foot, swarms of the nobility and gentry arrived, accompanied by " bathers of the lower class of society " bent, as it was presumed, on cleansing away " all the collected stains and impurities of the year." Their collected clamour for accommodation was the start of the hotel business and until suitable buildings could be rushed up early visitors would sleep out in the sandhills, beg shelter in barns and outbuildings, or share the already overcrowded beds of the local natives.

Within half a century, ancient Lytham had far outstripped Blackpool as a seaside resort, and for long years, relics of her past remained for all to see. The central pivot of the community was the market place into which the stage coaches were to rumble in, horns at full blast, with their passengers. To this spot, then as now triangular in shape, came the old fairs, with their hobby horses, coconut shies and swings. There the good wife, pump bound and bucket in hand, would pause to exchange the gossip of the day with a neighbour, to inspect new arrivals, to glean scraps of news from obliging coachmen. By 1837 the old fish-stones, where sales were conducted two or three times a week, had seen their better days, and Thomas Catterall of Kirkham volunteered to erect new ones . . . " to be 18 feet diameter (outside dimensions) by 2 feet wide . . . for the sum of eight pounds."

Nearby stood the village cross and the stocks, the entrance gates to the Hall Park (the railway obliged their removal to the present site), and the Market (now County & Commercial) Inn.

In 1846, Lytham's popularity was boosted by the arrival of the railway. Outlying villagers swarmed weekly into the township, and with prosperity nudging their elbows the Commissioners of the Lytham Improvement Act resolved in 1847 . . . " that the plot of land adjoining the Commercial Inn be selected as a site for a market house."

Mr. Reed of Liverpool prepared plans for a neat brick and stone building, and in 1848, at a cost of £1,000, the Market House went up. So did sand-grown eyebrows when the Saturday market crowds began to exceed the brightest expectations. No longer dependent upon the weather, shoppers now thronged the rectangular hall where twenty or more stalls peddled every possible type of consumer goods. There was something to tempt all ages, and the stall-holders did a roaring trade.

Thus, for 30 or 40 years, the Market House flourished. In 1868, generous-hearted Lady Eleanor Cecily Clifton decided to give a clock to the town . . . " which will be of great benefit to the inhabitants." The Commissioners placed the order with Cooke and Sons of York, and by 1872 the Market House tower had been raised to accommodate the town clock beneath which, in a room over the ornamental iron gates, the Improvement Commissioners regularly held their meetings. Except for this addition to the tower, and thanks to some skilful and sensitive restoration, the building still largely retains its original appearance of 1848.

Unfortunately, Lytham's increasing prosperity attracted an increasing number of private shops, barrow boys and hawkers. Trade at the Market House gradually dwindled, gloom descended upon one vacated stall after another, and shopping housewives transferred their custom to the more fashionable Clifton Street.

At length no choice remained but to convert this once prosperous and bustling hall into separate shops, to the everlasting regret of some of Lytham's old ones who well recalled the market in its heyday.

When the trams came even the old fairs could operate no longer on their traditional site, but had to move out of the town centre. Early this century there was colour and spectacle enough in the old market place when uniformed bands serenaded the shoppers.

After the First World War the site was laid out as a memorial to fallen " sandgrown 'uns," where now, in the midst of the traffic, one can sit in a quiet retreat, shaded by the majestic trees which, in 1850, were donated as saplings by the Squire of Lytham.

The Market House and Cenotaph, Lytham. (*Photograph by Alderman A. F. Williamson, C.C.*).

The ancient elm tree, known locally as Old Tom, which stood beside the village green (Cenotaph side), near fish-stones and stocks, and in front of the former entrance to Lytham Hall Park (now site of Clifton Estate Offices). *(Block kindly loaned by the artist, T. A. Clarke, Esq)*.

LYTHAM WINDMILL

I wonder how often Lytham Windmill has been sketched, painted, and photographed, and just how many family albums include holiday snaps taken of Mum and Dad and the kids against a background of this lovely old structure.

Philip Robinson described it aptly on Television as " Looking like a little bit of the country come up to the seaside for the day," and certainly it must come as a pleasant shock when a visitor for the first time spots this whitewashed windmill, rising up out of the green, and poking its arms proudly at the sky against a backcloth of the shimmering Ribble.

Read your history books and you will automatically conclude that the windmill has stood here for centuries. Your conclusions, however, will be wrong.

Certainly there were windmills in Lytham during the lifetime of the Benedictine Priory which functioned between 1190 and 1539. From the Durham records, we find that in 1327 the Prior granted part of the " waste " land to John de Bradkirk and his wife, and to their son for his lifetime, at a rental of 4d. per newly approved acre, on condition that the corn grown was ground at Lytham mill. A 17th century sketch of the township (see Page 13) shows a post windmill standing between Lytham Hall and the Church, and a map of 1786 indicates that two mills once stood on a site now enclosed within the Hall Park.

Even the late Allen Clarke, revered Lancashire Poet-Journalist and a noted authority on Fylde windmills, fell into the error of declaring Lytham's to be the " Daddy of all the Fylde windmills . . . the oldest of the lot," and adjudging it to have been built in 1762. Maybe he had been poking around amongst the machinery and discovering some dates there which completely misrepresented the true facts. Nowadays we have abundant evidence that mill machinery is toughly built and stands the test of time remarkably well. It would appear, therefore, that when, in 1805, Richard Cookson sought and obtained a lease from the Squire for a plot of land on Lytham " Marsh," on which to erect a " windy milne," he had previously bought up serviceable parts from other disused mills in the Fylde. The building of Lytham mill at this time was also confirmed in contemporary writings.

Comparatively youthful then, as it may seem, will anyone love it the less ? I doubt it. My only regret is that the sails now remain motionless though I can remember them revolving merrily in a high wind more than thirty years ago.

Originally, as can be seen from old prints of Lytham's early days, the mill sails were made of canvas. In 1845 we find a letter from one William Houghton of Kirkham to the miller . . . " If it be so that you want a sute of cloths for her I should be much obliged to you for the order, as I fit all in Preston and nearly all in the neighbourhood with mill sailcloths."

The windmill, on account of its exposed position, was solidly built on walls 5 feet thick at the base. It had a cellar and four storeys, and millstones 5 feet in diameter.

Sad days and bright days were all a part of its story, and a fatality occurred in 1909. A small boy, on a Manchester schoolchildren's outing, was tempted by the dipping blades. Then they were functional, rather than decorative as at present, and exaggerated in length. The lad was swept up aloft, but at the topmost reach he lost his nerve, and plunged headlong

Lytham Mill. (*Photograph by the late Douglas Brown*).

to sudden death. Yet countless grannies and grandads can recall picking daisies in the shade of the mill to the accompanying creak of gently revolving sails.

The mill, one of so many in the Fylde that Allen Clarke called it "Windmill Land," operated until 1918 when, on the first day of the year, it was ravaged by fire and put out of action. The interior was gutted, machinery crashed down, grain was destroyed and blazing timbers were scattered far and wide.

After the sad event the mill was bought up by the Local Authority, and in later years freshened up and given a new hat and a set of ornamental sails.

The building has served several purposes since then. It was a cafe for a while. Then the North-Western Electricity Board took it over and imaginatively set it to use as a sub-station. After that, the members of the Lytham Motor Boat Club, the Ribble Cruising Club, and the Sea Cadets, all at some time had entree to this attractive Ribble landmark whose beauty, it is to be hoped, will be adorning calendars, picture postcards, and family albums for centuries to come.

THE PASSING OF LYTHAM PIER

Look in vain for a pier at Lytham. On 4th March, 1960, they came along and started to tear it down. For weeks they worked, these demolition men, in the teeth of a piercing spring wind, and as the weather mellowed, the old iron lady that we had known for so long, had dwindled to nought.

" Lytham Pier is no good . . .
Chop it up for fire-wood ! "

Soon, how well the old jingle applied, we could see very clearly. They started with the pier approach, the wide expanse, flanked by two octagonal gatehouses, where Victorian crowds once assembled in profusion. Now the planks were torn up from their moorings and tossed into pathetic, jagged heaps. Motorists caught up the best bits, and raced home with a boot-ful, thinking in terms of firewood or fettling, whilst we, who loved the old pier, noticed only that the girders, now harshly exposed, were flaking with rust and decay.

After a few weeks only, the pier was gone, and Lytham's seafront wore the strangely shorn look of a ringleted lad emerging from his first appointment with the barber.

But on this spot, on the Easter Monday of 1865, the scene was very different. Then the crowds, brought in by excursions from all over Lancashire, thronged to support the delighted " sandgrown 'uns " in the business of opening their new pier.

The New Pier at Lytham (1865). (*From an old sketch*).

They had wanted one for a long time, and in 1861, the Pier Company had made so bold as to seek permission to build one . . . " at a cost of Six Thousand Pounds and no more ! " Three years went by before the first pile was screwed in, but soon the structure rose majestically from the sands of Lytham. And what a fine pier it was, too, an elegant piece of marine architecture which could only bring advantage to the town.

Now, you could walk along its 914 feet length, " for exercise, pleasure, or any other purpose," on payment of 2d. Airing the baby in his perambulator cost 4d., and an extra 6d. enabled you to perform the same service for Grandma, snugly enthroned in her " bath or sedan chair."

Local boatmasters had added reason to bless the pier. They could use it freely, for embarking or disembarking, by paying £1 per year, but no-one, for obvious reasons, could " ship or unship . . . any sheep, cattle or merchandise."

But first there was the opening ceremony, which was performed by Mrs. Clifton. Processions had marched through the town, bands had blown themselves almost breathless. Bunting flapped in the breeze, mayoral chains twinkled in the sunshine, and half the notables of the county had come to give the pier a good send-off. The lifeboat, gaily trimmed, led a nautical procession of fishing craft close to the shore, two corps of Volunteers drew crisply to attention, whilst at a neighbouring hotel luncheon " of an auspicious and gratifying character " was being prepared for the guests of the Company.

This was a day to remember and one that the " sandgrown 'uns " made haste to celebrate in right royal fashion. Lytham now had a pier, in an era when piers were very well thought of, and sea-going Victorian families would now be greatly convenienced when arriving or departing by steamer for such places as Preston, Blackpool, Southport . . . and places beyond.

This was only the beginning. A Floral Hall was added during the naughty 'nineties, and after that there was the new concert pavilion (which became later a roller skating rink, and finally a cinema). But there was a mishap in 1903 during an angry gale. Two barges slipped their moorings and sliced the pier in the middle, fortunately missing the pavilion which, however, went up in flames in 1927 and was never rebuilt.

The Floral Hall functioned with diminishing success until it was decided to close the pier altogether in 1938. And that was the beginning of the end.

During the last war, the wind, waves, and years of neglect, bit sorely into the old iron structure. Only the boatmen of Lytham, and the Trinity House pilots, were prepared to entrust their lives and limbs to the rotting timbers so beloved of the Victorians, and with every passing month the decay bit deeper.

At last it was decreed that " this potential danger to the public " must come down. There had been protests and public meetings. A Fighting Committee had striven desperately, but vainly, to keep the pier alive.

So, in the Spring and early Summer, we watched it diminishing steadily until nothing remained but a host of memories kept alive by the old ones. Of minstrel shows, and over-dressed crowds, and the clanging bell of the departing steamer. Of gas lamps twinkling in recesses along the decking and dancing like agitated glow-worms on the waves below ; of a pint-size foreign gentleman with a tasselled Tarboosh selling Oriental novelties and carved wooden beads ; of the rumble of roller skates, and the squeals ; of the silent, but wildly histrionic, heroines of the silver screen ; of banjoes strumming, and the wailing of the wind ; of salt spray flying, and seabirds calling, and the grim, relentless creeping of decay.

LYTHAM CLUB DAY

Every year, on a Midsummer Saturday, the people of Lytham celebrate their Annual Club Day. For this great event, thousands of people, from the Borough and beyond, flock into the township, thronging the streets, choking traffic off the roads, and suspending the local 'bus services.

A colourful carnival procession, seemingly endless, and rich with variety and spectacle, wends its way through the town to the merry music of several uniformed bands.

Even the visitors become caught up in the infectious holiday atmosphere of the affair, but for the genuine natives, Club Day has a special significance. It was the Great Day of the Year for their forefathers in an age when life was the sobering, and sometimes grim business of rearing large families in over-burdened cottages, and on insufficient wages. Pleasures in those days were few, and the excuse, for once, for merry-making and letting the hair down, was eagerly siezed upon by " sandgrown 'uns," whether young or old.

The children, on that day, received their yearly spending money . . . three pennies . . . and for a few brief hours felt like millionaires with a fortune to squander on the hobby horses and swings.   On Club Day morning they were up with the lark, and with untold wealth jingling in their pockets, were galloping along the lanes into Lytham as though they had wings to their boots.   " But Oh, dear me ! " as one octogenarian recalled, years ago, " when you had spent up and done for a year, it did seem a long way back home."

Nevertheless, whether by anticipation or in retrospect, the young of the parish enjoyed Club Day to the full, and it was a splash of vivid colour in a grey existence.

The older folk had their own reasons for looking forward to Club Day, but strangely enough, the event started off with the formation of temperance and friendly societies.   Once a year they paraded their strength, and their regalia through the town before moving on to a celebration meal.   Gradually, other organisations, the lifeboat crews, sportsmen, and day and Sunday school scholars began to join in the procession which grew in ambition and importance with the years, and there has been a Rose Queen since 1894.

In the early days, the old fairs, with their noise and sideshows and swings, set up their pitch in the triangular market place, but eventually traffic congestion caused them to move to a field not far removed from the town centre.   Nowadays, when the procession has dissolved away, most folk find themselves drifting towards the dusty, gusty clamour of this traditional fair.   And long after the crowning ceremony which, on so many happy occasions, has been performed by Mrs. Violet Clifton of Lytham Hall, the music blares out upon the June night air, and the old ones remember that it hasn't changed a bit since they and their grand-parents were young.

BLOW THAT SAND !

When the wind comes up fresh from the sea, every capricious gust lifts a fine spume of malicious needles to lash the cheeks and sting the eyes of pedestrians.   Motorists, peering out from frosted windscreens, note the whine and thump of the elements.   And the Borough Surveyor begins to reckon up the cost in terms of pounds, shillings, and pence.

It is a costly business these days to keep the Borough's roads clear of blown sand, amounting sometimes to more than £3,000 in a year.   Yet the town of St. Annes could never have existed but for this menace which plagued our forefathers, for the whole of that area consists of a peat bog overblown with sand.

Earlier during the century, the age-old problem was somewhat mitigated by the North Channel, or North Hollow, a wide channel of water which remained to a considerable depth at low tide and which, flowing in from Oliver's Heading, extended past St. Annes Pier and along the coast as far as Fairhaven Lake.

Partly as a result of the training walls, and partly from natural causes, the old waterway, where around the clock, steamers and private yachts could tie up near St. Annes Pier, became silted up and entirely disappeared.

But so long as it existed this expanse of water created an effective barrier to the flying particles of sand.

In addition, as was predicted by many of our public men years ago, the foreshore scheme, which was responsible for the removal of thousands of tons of shingle from our coast, must have aggravated an already tiresome situation.

On the other hand, pedestrians and picnic-parties in ever increasing numbers cannot be held blameless. Until Sir Alan Cobham's Air Circus came to thrill us all in the early days of flying, and until holidays with pay and every other man with a car in the garage to enable him to enjoy frequent trips to the seaside, the clumps of tough starr grass, whose binding roots securely anchored the sand, were left undisturbed.

The sand-dunes towards Squire's Gate then rose to such lofty heights as to obliterate any view of the sea from the upper deck of the old tramcars. When the work of the starr grass was sabotaged the giant golden mounds were gradually whittled down by the coquettish winds to below the level of the main road. Thus disappeared what might have proved an effective barrier to some future inundation of the sea.

(*Photograph by Alderman A. F. Williamson, C.C.*).

This business of blowing sand is no new problem. In Lytham in earlier centuries, that stretch of common land lying between the township and St. Cuthbert's Church earned the nickname of "Hungry Moor." Sand-blown and wind-tossed, this arid scrubland provided only meagre grazing for a handful of poor folks' cows, and going back even further, we come to the sorry plight of Thomas Dannett in the 16th century.

The Dissolution was at hand. The Benedictine Priory of Lytham was about to go the way of all others. In a last despairing attempt to evade confiscation, the Priors of Durham, from whom the Lytham cell had originally sprung, hastily rigged a lease with Thomas Dannett, gentleman, for all the Lytham possessions for a term of 80 years. (This piece of ecclesiastical sleight-of-hand, while it delayed, certainly did not ultimately deflect, the main course of events. By 1554 that Court hanger-on and " devourer of Monastic lands," Sir Thomas Holcroft, had clamped his avaricious hooks into Lytham).

But in 1549, having struggled during the ten years of his tenancy to support . . . " all that there house, church or manor of Lethum in the County of Lancaster, with all houses, lodgings, orchards, gardens, barns,

43

byres, stables, dovehouses, windmills, sheepcoates and all other edifices, buildings and houses of office whatsoever they be to the said place . . ." Thomas Dannett found himself in the embarrassing situation of being unable to pay his rent of £48 19s. 6d., because of damage, loss of use to land and buildings, etc., occasioned by " the rage of sand."

His youthful royal landlord, Edward VI, thereupon despatched his Chancellor and General Surveyor to investigate the claim, and sure enough, inspection revealed that four cottages and gardens, 5 acres of pasture, 99 of arable, 42 acres " letten to and amongst divers of the tenants of the said manor", 410 acres of common pasture and 28 acres of marsh, had been ravaged beyond reclaim through blown sand. In consequence, tenant Dannett was annually out of pocket to the tune of £22 11s. 4d., which sum otherwise he could have expected to draw in.

In addition to these grievous deprivations, " the capital house of the said Manor of Lethum " was found to be standing " in great danger by reason of the rage of sand there so that the same of necessity must shortly be taken down and set and builded in some other place."

Under these circumstances it is not surprising that Thomas Dannett found himself up to the neck in financial embarrassment. But his claim had been found to be just, and the monarch was inclined to be merciful. On 2nd July, 1549, by letters patent attested by Sir Richard Sackville, Knight of Westminster, the tenant of Lytham was " clearly acquitted, defaulted and discharged " of his arrears, and annually excused all but the sum of £26 15s. 7½d., plus an annual payment of 40s. to cover priest's wages and bailiff's fees.

Whatever their reactions all those years ago, there might have been some sort of cold comfort for the Lythamers of Tudor times had they known that their descendants, in the progressive and sophisticated 20th century, would still be scratching their heads over the same age-old problems.

A WORLD APART—HEYHOUSES AND THE WEST END

THE ORATORY OF KILGRIMOL

For hundreds of years the name of Kilgrimol has charged imagination in these parts with mystery, romance, and some confusion.

" It was a church," they will tell you, the old ones who claim to know. " Only, it was swamped by the sea, and buried. On New Year's Eve, though, or when a storm is brewing up out there, the bell can still be heard tolling from under the waves ! "

The story, heavily embroidered, and with infinite variations, has been told and re-told on a thousand winter nights beside cottage hearths. Some of our " sandgrown " families have been great raconteurs down the centuries, for in humble homes they cultivated the art of story-telling and conversation to a high degree, and no subject can ever have been so mulled over as the Oratory of Kilgrimol.

One version, taken to extreme limits, tells of a penitent cell set up on a wave-lashed sandbank, to which nefarious priests were despatched and left to deliberate upon their wrong doings until liberated by the next tide. But this is only one version, and there have been many.

Discounting all the fancies of the imagination, however, no-one seriously denies, these days, that Kilgrimol did exist. A map of the district, c.1532, clearly records the name " Kylgmoles " in a position which, allowing for all discrepancies, must have stood along the coast between St. Annes and Squire's Gate.

Going back even further in time, to the setting up of the Benedictine Priory in 1190, by Richard Fitz Roger, we find mention in the Foundation Charter of a boundary cross having been set up . . . " on the western side of the cemetery of Kilgrimol." It was this cross which was to give its name in later centuries to the hamlet of Cross Slack whose tumbled ruins can still be seen on St. Annes Old Links.

But what of the Oratory itself, for a tradition as persistent as Kilgrimol is rarely without some foundation in fact. In the centuries before the Conquest, we know that Celtic missionaries were active in these parts, and even without a specific mention in Domesday, it is now widely accepted that a church functioned within the Manor of Lytham before the Survey.

It might well have been an insignificant foundation, limited to a burial ground and a mud or wooden hut to shelter the priest. But " The Legend of the Lost Brother " presents a different picture, recalling the days when Amounderness was massively afforested, rich in swamp, and abounding with red deer, wild oxen, badgers, foxes, and all the creatures of the woodland.

On a violent winter's night, we are told, and with a giant tide running before the wind, the sea rose up in a wrath, boiled over the land, and battered down the firs and oaks of the forest. Then, Oswald, the Gentle Prior of Kilgrimol, gathered in the inhabitants and animals of the forest to shelter within his walls. When all were safe he climbed a hillock and turned his eyes upon a scene of awful destruction.

For days, and long months, and longer years after the inundation, the crippled trees lay creaking and dying in a salt-ridden swamp, and when the sand blew, and laid an ever-thickening mantle over the place, it became in time as though the forest had never existed. Instead, there emerged the Cornfield of Amounderness which gave its name to the Fylde. But near to that place ever after was known as " The Blowing Sands."

A romantic legend ? A figment of a too-lively sand-grown imagination ? Tradition, again, says different, and insists that the priests who served Kilgrimol were of the Culdee Order.

The Culdees, of Irish origin, and founded during the 8th century, were moderately active in Scotland and her Isles, at York, and along these northern coasts. Their life was one of simplicity, self-sacrifice, and personal service. They cared nothing for temporal possessions, and territorially were entirely without ambition. Maybe it is on account of these negative virtues that one hears so little of their activities in England.

When King Athelstan of Northumbria journeyed northwards around 930 A.D. to do battle, he called, as was the custom, at the Church of St. Peter in York to ask a blessing on the venture. There he would see the faithful Culdee brethren ministering to the sick, the lepers, and the poor. When victory had been secured, in gratitude he bestowed Amounderness upon the Church, and it is certainly not beyond possibility that one or two Culdee priests were despatched here to minister to the needs of the community.

The name, Culdee, was derived from words meaning " Companions, or Servants of God." They were dedicated men. They sought nothing for themselves. But whatever the reason, the Church at York speedily returned the gift, possibly on account of its inaccessibility. Yet a small nucleus of Culdees could have remained to continue their godly service to the community.

There have been many conjectures as to the probable date of Kilgrimol. It is doubtful now whether any documentary evidence still survives to set the scene accurately in time. During the last thousand years, however, there have been numerous and regular inundations of the sea. Our coastline has changed beyond recognition, and many feet of golden blown sand have accumulated over the long past.

Nevertheless, one can confidently predict that the Oratory of Kilgrimol will continue to intrigue and tantalise the historians of the future as it has continually engaged those of the past.

Before the First World War, the Rev. W. T. Bulpit, late Vicar of Crossens and a noted Lancashire antiquary, paid many visits to the cottages of Cross Slack. He propounded the pretty theory that the threshold stone of Granny Fisher's cottage had been the base of the old boundary cross. Unfortunately for him, the cottage was then in the full flourish of life. Tampering with the foundations would have brought the old homestead crashing in ruins—which is precisely what wind and weather, and absence of human warmth, have done since that time.

Perhaps one of these days someone will seek permission to investigate further, and if they do, they will like to be reminded that Mrs. Edward Fisher, who died aged 88 during the 1920's, remembered her husband, when ploughing years before, turning up a collection of large stones. Examination established them to be of imported mill-stone grit, and the Rev. Bulpit and the late Mr. James Bowman, one-time Editor of the *Lytham St. Annes Express* and himself a keen local historian, carried the stones and carefully laid them in the cottage garden against future investigations. Time passed, no-one bothered, and the stones finished up being tossed into the bottom of an old well.

One cannot hear of such occurrences without harking back immediately to the Oratory of Kilgrimol in whose burial ground, now lying under the tenth fairway, not only were local inhabitants interred, but also the bodies of unknown shipwrecked seamen, washed up on the beach very regularly in times of storm.

Perhaps one of these days we shall know the full story of vanished Kilgrimol. Until then, one man's story is as good as another's, and if it tells of significant shadows on the greens, and of bells tolling under the sea, so much the better. It will be a poor day for us all when we fail to be held spell-bound and open-mouthed by colourful tales from the past.

CROSS SLACK, A HAMLET THAT DIED

From the top of Highbury Road bridge you catch sight of them in the distance, the ruined cottages of the once flourishing little hamlet of Cross Slack. From a railway train travelling between St. Annes and Squire's Gate you can clearly see them nestling in the midst of St. Annes Old Links.

Probably three centuries ago, they sprang up, close to the sea which

View from the train in the old days. (*Greatly enlarged from a photograph by Frank Dean, Esq.*).

provided a livelihood, and near to the burial ground of Kilgrimol in which local folk and the bodies of shipwrecked seamen from long times were interred.

This was the extreme end of the old parish of Lytham. Lytham was severed from the Manor of Layton by Division Lane of which remains can be traced over the little hump-backed railway bridge, and which, travelling seawards, dissolves into the sand immediately before Squire's Gate Camp.

That this is Kilgrimol territory is borne out by a map of 1532 which was drawn when trouble broke out between the Layton and Lytham tenants. And not for the first time, mark you ! For centuries there had been squabbles about boundaries and wreck-rights, and cattle eating someone

47

else's grass and people building houses on someone else's ground ! Hopeless confusion seems to have arisen from small personal bequests of land on Layton Hawes to the Benedictine Priory of Lytham in the early days of its existence, and though the Priors were only asserting what they considered to be their rights, they did so only under the baleful eye of Layton's Lord.

In 1338 Widow Sybil Butler aggravated an already ticklish situation by sneaking into the Lytham domain and dragging an anchor just over the border into Layton to enrich her Manor to the extent of the wreck salvage. Trivial acts of this nature kept local feelings running high and there was no love lost between the " sandgrown 'uns " and those whom they were pleased to call the " mossogs " on the other side of the boundary.

The year 1530 saw the flare-up of an unseemly brawl when " 100 riotous persons " from the Layton (Marton Moss) area rose to the support of Dame Margaret Butler and her son, rampaged over priory lands, set about Lawrence Billington's house and in so doing " cast out valuable goods, pulled all the buildings down and cut the timber into pieces." Another " riotous band " helped themselves to 100 loads of rushes (for thatching), destroyed ditches and fencing, and drove the cattle amongst growing corn.

Threatened with having his house pulled down about his ears, the Prior fled and there descended an uneasy peace which was to be rudely shattered

Granny Fisher's Cottage. (*Photograph by Alderman A. F. Williamson, C.C.*).

when, two years later, 200 armed Layton tenants converged upon the Lytham border and set about their destructive work with a will.

It was at this point that the Chancellor of the Duchy of Lancaster intervened to restore order and to try to assess the rights of the case. The map was prepared, depositions were taken, and though some doubts still lingered as to whether or not some former Prior had been responsible for a piece of

48

monastic fiddling, the case was found in favour of the Benedictines. But at least a sort of hostile truce was declared and there were no more physical onslaughts. Division Lane, however, which long before the extension of the aerodrome was a mere cart track running the full length of the Lytham boundary, now sharply divided the two communities as effectively as a one-hundred foot chasm, and in some quarters a lingering coolness still remains to this day. At any rate, the name of " Mad Nook " serves to remind us of the vigorous local skirmish which took place long centuries ago.

The Cross Slack cottages were built within sight of a 12th century boundary cross. The word " Slack " possibly comes from the old Norse "slakki," meaning a shallow dell ; the Scottish " slack " means a boggy place, a cleft between hills. In this area throughout the ages water collected into natural hollows, and froze over in the winter, providing the " sandgrown 'uns " with a ready-made skating arena ; even to this day, close to the cottages is a pond which never dries up.

Nowadays, since the people went away and left the houses to die, and since the wind, weather and the vandals have wrought their mischief, it is perhaps difficult to picture the cottages in their heyday. Half a lifetime ago, and a good deal less, they presented a bonny sight with their trim thatches, white walls, and warmth and life spilling out from their tiny windows and doors.

Here was the sort of existence which has largely disappeared from man's ken. Oil lamps, and well water, fires of dusty dried turf, and the delicious smell of home baked bread. The stunted trees might bend and creak and stretch their pleading arms away from the wind, but the cobble walls of the old cottages stood stout and weatherproof, sheltering long generations of sturdy " sandgrown 'uns." They worked hard and they lived long, these folk, unless infection nipped them harshly in infancy. At eleven they left school and matured into men and women overnight, bringing home a

Nancy's, or Keeper's Cottage. (*Photograph by Donald Cardwell, Esq.*).

pittance to eke out the family budget. Always the problem was where to sleep these large families who somehow managed to grow up in the incredibly cramped quarters beneath the thatch.

In the most intact of the cottages Granny Fisher last reared her family of eleven, cooked and provided for them in a miniature kitchen with an inconveniently low ceiling, and watched the children climbing the cat ladder and snuggling beneath the blankets in the warm corners beside the chimney upstairs.

Certainly to the womenfolk fell the hardest lot, of making ends meet, of coping with frequent childbirths, of portering all the family provisions, and of enduring the tedium of life in an isolated community.

Far from market and church, even the passage of an Estate cart provided a welcome distraction, and it was a red letter day when Lady Eleanor Cecily Clifton called in on her rounds to enquire about the children, to bring gifts of food and warm clothing, and to inspire a feeling of "belonging" in the forgotten folk of Cross Slack.

For the men there was always the cheering prospect of a convivial evening at the Trawl Boat to lighten a long day's care, and when feet dragged after the day's toil, there was always Nancy's nearer at hand.

Nancy's, or Keeper's Cottage, stood nearby on Division Lane, and in this last outpost of the Lytham Manor lived the gamekeeper who endeavoured, however unsuccessfully, to discourage the locals from bagging a Sunday dinner at the Squire's expense.

Nancy's was a great calling place to which visitors came on foot, or on horseback. There were cobbles on the westerly wall for the hanging of saddles and bridles, and within the cottage there was always a draught of Nancy's home-brew to refresh the thirsty. There, making his rounds, the Clifton Agent would frequently call and raise his elbow before cantering back to Lytham along the beach, and workmen from the Estate lost no chance of making a detour by way of the defiantly white little cottage.

Now Nancy's too has gone the way of all the others, and lies a tumbled mass of cobbles beside the old well where once gushed the sweetest water, and in a place where once was abundant laughter and life.

CROSS SLACK FARM IN HIGHBURY ROAD

This lovely old homestead, now within hailing distance of St. Annes Old Links Clubhouse and with masses of contemporary brick jostling its elbows and breathing down its neck, once stood in splendid isolation.

To this day, however, it remains as beautiful as at any time during almost three centuries of existence. This long-time home of the Gillett family, with its wind-tossed trees and shrubs, and surrounding cobble wall, was once a farmhouse of some substance attached to a community of small cots.

Such changes as have been made to its structure have so mellowed with time that it is difficult to picture the building in the original. The windows were smaller and sported tiny bulls-eye panes. Entrance through the westerly wall was protected from the boisterous sea-winds by an old barn which was attached to the shore-wards side of the house. In 1796 this western door was cobbled up (the signs were perfectly visible until very recently), the old barn was demolished, and a new and far grander one, with huge timbered beams, was erected to the landward. A kitchen and back door were added to the rear of the house.

The old walls never gleamed more whitely than they do at this present time, and no thatch was ever neater. Nowadays Mr. Gillett uses the wiry starr grass which withstands the weather quite as effectively as the straw used in olden times and which, moreover, discourages the destructive inclinations of the birds.

It is a labour of love to Old Bill to trudge across the dunes selecting the spiky strands to suit the job, and much of his life is spent perched upon his well-used ladders. But his work shines forth for all to see and enjoy, and whether splashed with whitewash, or busy drying the dishes, Bill Gillett (he is unmarried and " batches " for himself) has always time to break off for a yarn. Stirring tales of the past come tumbling as if by nature from this brilliantly blue-eyed son of the sand, whose ancestors farmed Cross Slack through long generations, and whose own clear memories are infused with those of his forbears.

Cross Slack Farm with Bill Gillett (right) and his brother. (*Photograph by Alderman A. F. Williamson, C.C.*).

On the settle in his spacious parlour have rested many illustrious folk, royalty not excluded, just to listen to the tales of long ago. And there is a lovely story told about his father, the late Mr. George Gillett, who was asked what he thought about this new-fangled electricity when it was first installed.

" Eeh ! It's grand," was the verdict. " Tha presses a waart on th't'wall, and th'leet comes on in a bottle up on th't'ceiling ! "

51

Mr. George Gillett, a bearded " sandgrown 'un," was born in 1851 into a family of seven, in one of the Twiggy Lane tied cottages. He lived to a ripe old age, was a " mine of memories," and even into his eighties still rose at 5 a.m. to milk the cows and put in a vigorous day's work around the farm.

He remembered, during his childhood, that his father received 9s. a week, a farm labourer's wages during the summer. The winters were spent " house-thacking," and scraping by on any odd jobs that came to hand. Driftwood and dried turf stoked the family fires, and after a porridge and milk breakfast it was bacon for dinner every day except for the Sunday joint. As a lad of twelve, Mr. George Gillett sat on a sandbank and watched the first lighthouse fall in 1863. When he was 19, his father took over Cross Slack, and upon his father's death it was handed on to the son.

Farmer though he had been all his days, Mr. George Gillett was still closely connected with the sea. He remembered many wrecks which benefited the sand-grown families who were quickest off the mark. From the " Susan Campbell " came barrels of bitter ale ; from the " Annie Cooper " a plentiful supply of tobacco ; the " Reuben " wreck littered the shore with timber ; and from the " Crusader " came . . . no-one was ever told what ! The local fishermen went there boring to see what they could find, but the old " sandgrown 'uns " could be as tight-lipped as the next man when it came to " th'upping," and certainly not all the bounty of the sea was handed over to the authorities !

Gillett's Crossing, the small railway halt at Highbury Road, was named after this family at Cross Slack. Local trains stopped on request, and the guard lowered a wooden ladder so that passengers could climb in. The keys of the crossing gates were kept at the farmhouse, and Estate carts, going down to the beach for another load of cobbles, would cross the railway lines at this point.

Old Mr. Gillett's lifetime stretched back to the days of simplest living, when local families went to bed without locking their doors, and one suit of working clothes comprised a youth's whole wardrobe. Luxuries were unheard of, necessities were cut down to the minimum. People walked further, worked harder, and managed without amusements. Yet very often they lived into healthy old age, and Mr. George Gillett needed a doctor for the first time in his life at the age of 77.

Now, of course, Old Bill is the last of the Gillett's at Cross Slack Farm, and with no son to continue in the old tradition one wonders how long this beautiful old gem of a place can survive. This, surely, must be an instance where the whole of the community will rise up with one loud and insistent voice to declare " HANDS OFF ! ! ! " if anyone should ever become insensitive enough to talk of destroying this lovely link with the long past.

THE OLD SCHOOL AT HEYHOUSES

Imagine that this is a fine summer's day in 1870, and that we are setting out for a walk from the point where School Lane forms a cross-roads with Common Lane.

Long ago, Common Lane was so named because it skirted that vast tract of land, stretching out to the foreshore, which from ancient times was set aside for common use by the inhabitants. They paid no rent to the Lord of the Manor, but could freely use the grazing, cut turf for fuel, and grow food supplies for the family. (Commonside, at Ansdell, still retains the old connection, though a previous generation frequently referred to the whole stretch as " th'owd looan ").

In 1873 St. Anne's Church will be built, and Common Lane, leading to it, will gradually become known as Church Road. But in 1870 there is as yet no church, no Heyhouses School on the opposite corner, and the little white gamekeeper's cottage (which was adjacent to both until recent months) is in the prime of its life. On the right (Beauclerk Gardens) we see Daddy Whiteside's farm, whitewashed and thatched. There lives Milk Jinny who is on cordial terms with Lady Eleanor Cecily, and who greets her august visitor thus informally : " Eeeh ! Tha's comed ageean, Woman ! Well, cum on in, an' I'se find thee a dish o' tay ! " (Common Lane is as often called " Milk Jinny's Looan ").

School Lane obviously derives its name from a seat of learning, and a few minutes' walk away in the distance we can see a low whitewashed building where it is safe to assume that the young of the district are being grounded in the Three R's.

With our backs to the sea, we saunter, between high hawthorns, along a narrow little lane which, one day, will become St. Annes Road East. At

Old Heyhouses School. (*Photograph by Frank Dean, Esq.*).

present, though, there is no hint of such significant development. Huge fields full of daisies stretch out on both sides of this tall-hedged track, and the children often call it Daisy Lane. On the left is the campfield of the Preston Militia who, along with other Volunteer Corps, come here for summer exercises every year. We can hear the men talking and laughing, and the occasional blast from a bugle, and the wind wafts an appetising smell from the direction of the cookhouse.

But we are making for the school which a year ago (1869) was rebuilt to a more commodious plan. Mind you, there had been a Heyhouses

School long before that. It all started in 1720 when a high tide and a wild storm brought the sea swirling over the land, not only on this part of the coast, but also across the Ribble, and in the Cockerham area. In Lytham, this disastrous inundation " broak down and washed away the bancks rampets and sea fences," overflowed the land, 40 houses and farm buildings, " doeing very great damage." A subscription fund for the relief of the stricken in several districts brought only a meagre £100 to the aid of the Lythamers, and no-one was brave enough to try and share out the spoils.

In the end, much to everyone's credit and public-mindedness, the money was set aside for the schooling of poor children, and the fund was increased in after years by small bequests in local wills.

From this small nucleus the Lytham Charities prospered and increased, and in 1729, the Trustees appointed a Mr. James Silcock " to teach a free school " which stood . . . " as well as possible in a dry and healthy situation about two stone casts from the sea shore," and presumably near the town centre.

Within a man's lifetime it proved inadequate, and when Mr. Thomas Clifton was requested to enlarge it, he responded by building a new school within Lytham Hall Park, in 1793. Eventually its presence so near the hall must have become irksome and it was pulled down in 1809. Its successor was built in that year on the site of the present St. Cuthbert's School in Church Road, Lytham.

This was all very well for the poor children of the township, quite a number of whom received a sound primary education, on their own door-step, and at the expense of the Charities. It was quite a different matter for the remoter youngsters of the parish who, by distance alone, were often debarred from any formal education.

Cottages on old Common Lane (Church Road) near Worsley Road, Ansdell. (*From a water colour by the late Walter Eastwood, reproduced by kind permission of Norman Stirrup, Esq , A.R.I.B.A., Chartered Architect*).

This picture was taken in front of the Convent of the Cross and Passion on East Beach (now St. Paul's Nursing Home) and clearly shows St. Peter's Sunday School in the Club Day Procession of 1907.

Club Day, 1907, with St. Peter's Sunday School scholars passing along East Beach.

The Scout Guard of Honour betokens that this picture is of the Rose Queen Elect on the occasion of Lytham's Club Day and Rose Queen Festival in the early years of the century. The scene is at the junction of Bannister Street and East Beach. The fancy fanlight over the doorway of the house on the right is still there, but sadly its twin from next door has gone missing.

Lytham Club Day, St. John's Church tableau in St. John's Street in 1905

From the records of the Lytham Charities, it appears that, by 1780, some faint attempt had been made to educate a few poor girls at Heyhouses, but in 1832, at a cost of £150, a new school was built there with provision for " as well boys as girls." Under the rules and regulations drawn up by the Trustees, " no child shall be admitted . . . who hath not a perfect knowledge of its letters " . . . " all boys . . . shall be removed on their attaining to the age of 9 years " . . . " twice a year each child shall pay to the Teacher one penny for brooms or brushes for sweeping and cleansing the school room," and the holidays were confined to three days at Easter, two days at Whitsuntide, and " two whole weeks at Midsummer and Christmas."

Scholars paid a penny a week for learning " writing and accounts " (arithmetic), an extra penny a week for " knitting and sewing," and sixpence a year " fire money " for providing fuel for the premises.

No doubt, for every child enrolled at the school, there were others whose parents either would not, or could not, raise the " school pence." Children from seven years of age upwards were frequently removed from the school during the summer months to help with jobs around the farm. In the middle of this (19th) century nine-year-old boys left school altogether and spent the rest of their lives in full time employment. It was only as the decades moved on that it became common for the children to stay on until the ripe old age of ten or eleven.

The Trustees were authorised to expend £200 on alterations and improvements at the old Heyhouses School in 1863, and the site was freely transferred to them by The Squire.

Still the accommodation proved inadequate, and last year (1869) they pulled the old school down and built us this new one. It is all on one floor, whitewashed, and slated. There seems to be no shortage of scholars though the oldest cannot be more than ten, or eleven. In one room there is a singing lesson in full swing, and the accompaniment is provided by the Headmaster who is seated at the old harmonium. Through the next window we see a class of solemn ten-year old girls struggling to master the difficult art of making button-holes look neat . . . and further on, the " babies " are reciting their multiplication tables in a sing-song drone.

Soon it will be time for home, and the older children will be dragging the young ones by the hand. Some will face a long walk, as far as Cross Slack, or even to Ansdell. But the headmaster is more fortunate. His cottage, and the gamekeeper's, are only a few yards away.

This is the year 1870. Some of these lively schoolboys will grow up to become victims in the " Mexico " disaster. All of them will spend their lifetimes either messing about in small boats or toiling on neighbouring farms.

One day there will be a church for these children . . . and perhaps a very much bigger and better school (which they will be building, and calling " Heyhouses School " in 1880, though we do not know it yet) . . . and some even say there will be horseless carriages and fine houses. Only then, of course, there will be no fields of daisies . . . and the militia will go elsewhere, if they still exist. And in 1959 they will come along and demolish this little school altogether, and all that will be left will be a pile of rubble and tumbled bricks, and the last lingering memories of a dying generation.

Butcher's Farm (now demolished) and Whiteside's Farm in background. (*Photograph by Frank Dean, Esq.*).

Saltcotes cottages (on right), (*From a water colour by the late Walter Eastwood, reproduced by kind permission of Norman Stirrup, Esq., A.R.I.B.A., Chartered Architect*).

VANISHED COTTAGES

Years ago, the late Mr. Harry Melling used to talk to me about Butcher's farm, on the corner of Kilnhouse Lane and Blackpool Road, and Whiteside's farm at the West End. Both the houses were originally long, low, cobble-and-thatch cottages. Some time during last century they were rebuilt on more commodious lines.

In June of this year (1960), the demolition men arrived to tear down Butcher's farmhouse. Having passed this whitewashed place literally thousands of times during recent years, it suddenly became a matter of pressing urgency to make a detailed inspection, for within a fortnight even the rubble had been removed and all that remained was the bare site.

By that time, however, I had established that Butcher's, like so many of the local farmhouses, was in fact a cottage within a house. The original flag-floored, two-bay cottage, was about 33 feet long, outside dimensions, with a small adjoining shippon or stable at the easterly end. Earlier families slept in the bower, or on an open platform supported on stilts, and lived in the hall in which, very often, a huge fire-hood swept down from the roof apex, projected over the hearth, and dominated the whole building.

There is a fine example of an old firehood still in existence at the Saltcotes cottage (now scheduled for demolition). When I visited the last occupant there, in 1958, the cottage was bright and twinkling with life. On either side of the firehood was a soot-loft, a wide shelf where most of the family lumber was deposited, to the increased hazard of fire. The front door opened directly on to the fireplace and the draught was diffused by a high-backed fireside settle.

The living room remained, as of old, open to the roof, but the bower had been divided at some time into kitchen offices with a quaintly-shaped bed-room overhead, lighted by a gable end window.

Mrs. Cottam (blind in later years, though no brasses ever shone more brilliantly than hers) had come to the cottage as a young bride sixty years earlier. Her husband, during his lifetime, regularly fettled the thatch and whitened the walls, and the cottage was a showpiece attracting architects, historians, and coaches laden with sightseers.

In May of this year, however, I called again at the empty Saltcotes cottage. It was a dying house. The plaster, mixed with straw, was begin-ning to flake away from the old firehood. Wallpaper was hanging in shreds. I made a farewell tour of this once beautiful little home which, at a conservative estimate. has stood in its present form for almost three centuries but which, undoubtedly, was built over the remains of an earlier house going back to Tudor times, and came away reflecting gleefully that, when they try to take it down, they will not have it all their own way !

As was proved at Butcher's farm, these cobble walls, often 18 ins. thick, present a pretty tough proposition. There, the modern bricks flaked off like fragments of biscuit and fell at a gentle nudge from the powerful machine. But the gable wall of the cottage within the house defied all attempts to chip it away, and after much persuasion, it fell over in a solid mass.

" They knew how to make cement in those days," was the contractor's comment. This they will soon discover at Saltcotes when they clear the site for the widening of the road.

Of the ancient Common Lane (Church Road) cottages remaining until just before the last war, perhaps the best remembered stood on the corner

Saltcotes Cottages. (*Block kindly loaned by Historic Society of Lancashire and Cheshire*).

Cottage on Church Road, corner of Smithy Lane, on site now occupied by modern dwellings. (*From a water colour by the late Walter Eastwood, reproduced by kind permission of Norman Stirrup, Esq., A.R.I.B.A., Chartered Architect*).

of Smithy Lane (opposite the War Memorial Homes). It had a wind-lashed orchard, and a productive vegetable garden, and callers in the old days were many. Horse brasses shone from the large chimney piece, and throughout there was an atmosphere of cheerfulness and cosy warmth. Again, when the people left it, it fell into swift decay, and its tumbling walls stood, as if in mute reproach, for many a long year, until the site was wanted again for post-war building.

At the corner of Northhouses Lane, where Moss Hall Lane branches off to the right, there is a whitewashed stable which once was a cottage home. The Richardson family lived there at the beginning of this century, and though some of our old " sandgrown 'uns " would not swear to it, they seemed to recall that earlier generations at this cottage slept on an open cockloft, under the thatch.

In Twiggy Lane (Highbury Road) two small tied cottages presented a picturesque sight until just before the first world war. For centuries they looked out over the common (now shops and houses in Headroomgate Road and district), and because of the wildness of the sea-winds their gable ends stood proud of the thatch. This was a common precaution along the Fylde coast, one which prevented many a roof from being whisked off in a gale but which, at the same time, gave our old cottages a distinctly sagging appearance.

The rent was never more than 1s. 6d. a week, and there were no rates. The occupants kept a cow or two, and a few chickens, and let them all roam freely along the green lanes. No-one objected so long as they were kept out of rented fields and did no damage to crops.

A few hundred yards further up the lane was Twiggy Hill farm, a place of some substance, with a small front garden enclosed within an old cobble wall. At one time there were two staircases in the one house, indicating conversion from two cottages, and the varying heights of the downstairs windows supports the theory of alterations having been made at different periods.

At " The Elms " in Heyhouses Lane, there is a fine example of the mating of cobble and brick. The original low house must have been one of considerable importance. It stood in a large and attractive old world garden, and five wells supplied the needs of the tenant farmer. At a later stage the roof was taken off and a whole new first floor was built on in hand-made brick. " The Elms " then assumed its present imposing proportions, and in addition to the family staircase, there was another for the use of the servants. Later again this large residence was divided between two families who, by pre-arrangement and the simultaneous withdrawing of bolts, could make a neighbourly call in a cloudburst without getting their feet wet.

The late Mr. J. C. Fairchild, a keen local historian and tenant of " The Elms " until recent times, was always amused by the sloping floors, especially the one leading to the front entrance, which might have been designed to speed the parting guest. A gentle push at the right moment was enough to send the departing caller hurtling through the front door at a gallop !

The large white front gate at " The Elms " was obviously designed for a more leisured age. Not all that many years ago it opened out into the road, (nowadays such a procedure would have some interesting results !), but with the increase of mechanical traffic it was thought wise to have it re-hung to open inwards.

A few minutes' walk along the lane, between " The Elms " and the Trawl Boat, there remained until after the war perhaps the most beautiful of all our local cottages. It was a 17th century gem of a farmhouse which in

Twiggy Lane Cottages. *(From a water colour " A Spring Morning," by the late Harold Partington, 1907, reproduced by courtesy of Mrs. J. C. Fairchild).*

Twiggy Hill Farm, the Anyon family and Old Bella, the spaniel. *(From a photograph kindly loaned by Mrs. Wm. Pearson).*

Fancy Lodge Cottages.

Lighthouse Keeper's Cottage, St. Annes.

later years was converted into two cottages. It had a front porch, three dormer windows, and a roof immaculately thatched. There was a large garden with an old pear tree and a vegetable plot at the rear, and tall trees protected this bonny homestead from the harsh winds of winter.

Hauntingly beautiful though it remained to the end, yet the tragedy of a doomed family named Warbrick still hovered about the walls of Fancy Lodge. In the summer of 1885 a young father and six of his children were fatally struck down after eating tainted pork, and within six weeks the last of the victims had been carried to the St. Annes Parish Churchyard.

At the beginning of this century, Mrs. Scott (now white-haired), of the Trawl Boat, moved with her husband and young family into Fancy Lodge, and still she carries happy memories of the fifteen years spent there in the larger of the two cottages. The ceilings were low, but so was the ground floor which could occasionally become inundated in a sudden deluge. Lighting and cooking were done by paraffin lamps and stoves, and Pilling and Blackpool dealers regularly came over the boundary selling peat for cottage fires. " Twenty-ten a penny ! " . . . their cries could be heard throughout our country lanes. There was a piped water supply from 1901 when the mains linking Ballam with St. Annes were linked up at Heyhouses.

In 1939 Fancy Lodge was condemned for human habitation, and the North Western Electricity Board took it over and used it as a sub-station. During the post-war building boom, however, this attractive site was wanted for a modern bungalow. Fortunately the trees were spared, where the rooks still nest, and the front garden wall still borders the roadside.

Some time in the middle of last century two cottages were built in the sandhills near Riley Avenue and Clifton Drive, to accommodate the lighthouse-keeper and a gamekeeper from the Clifton Estate. The first lighthouse operated from 1847-1863, and the second from 1865-1901. It is obvious from the picture that housing standards had risen considerably by that time, and the two new cottages (whitewashed and slated), were stoutly built, lofty, and comparatively large.

Whatever the inconveniences and inadequacies of the old cottages of the parish of Lytham, most people are inclined to agree that nothing compares with them nowadays for sheer charm and beauty. They blended in with the landscape, they just naturally belonged to the place, and it is at least some consolation to have memories of them recalled in pictures.

SAND-GROWN FAMILIES AND A FORGOTTEN WAY OF LIFE

Hard work, plenty of exercise, simple food, and a mind uncluttered by too much book-learning—this was the lot which fell to the typical " sand-grown 'un " in the old days. His pleasures were few and far between. Lytham Club Day was for him the outstanding excitement of the year, whether he lived in the township, or in the wilds of the undeveloped West End. He thought nothing of walking to Preston, or Poulton, to mingle with the crowds at markets and fairs, and if he missed the train home from Blackpool he would stretch his legs sooner than wait for the next.

The heaviest burden undoubtedly fell, during these hard times, upon the harassed housewife and mother. The marriage might produce a score of

Cottage (now demolished) in North Houses Lane, Heyhouses. (*Block kindly loaned by the artist, T. A. Clarke, Esq.*)

children, not all of whom lived, but a goodly proportion of whom often had to be housed and reared in three or four low-ceilinged, cramped little rooms.

In 1860, for instance, it was estimated that, on the average, 12 people were living in every house in Lytham, but we know that numbers far in excess of the round dozen often crowded the ancient cottages handed down from a long past.

Mellings Lane was named after the old sand-grown family who had long lived in the two whitewashed cottages there. They now overlook the new Queensway, they are scheduled for demolition, and, by present standards, they look incredibly small.

Two brothers rented the cottages, and lived there with their families. Another brother had been unsuccessfully seeking accommodation, and the two tenants put their heads and, literally, their cottages together, knocked an extra door in at the back, and made three cottages out of two.

This private domestic arrangement went completely unnoticed at the Estate Office. Every week the rent-clerk knocked on the two front doors, collected 1/-d. from each, and went off quite satisfied and completely unaware of the third door round at the rear.

This, perhaps, would scarcely seem to merit a mention until one realises that one brother had seven children ; the second had eleven ; and the third had seventeen !

Imagine, if you can, the plight of a woman thus burdened. Coal, which

Mellings Lane Cottages. (*Photograph by Frank Dean, Esq*).

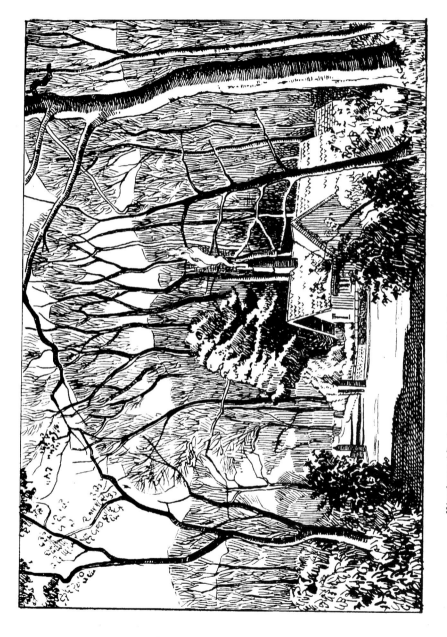

Watchwood Lodge. Lytham.   (*Block kindly loaned by the artist, T. A. Clarke, Esq*).

cost only coppers a bag, was out of her reach. Her husband and the boys went to the farthest field in Kilnhouse Lane to cut squares of turf for fuel. Faggots from the plantation, or driftwood from the beach, supplied the rest.

Yet, somehow, all the family bread had to be baked in the tiny iron oven by the heat of this hissing, spitting blaze which could never be allowed to go out and all the water for cleansing and family laundry had to be heated in the set-pot. Not, however, before it had been laboriously wound up, carried, and poured in, bucketful by bucketful, from the old well out in the garden.

Paraffin lamps and candles lit the cottages, and it was a disaster of the first magnitude if Lamp Oil Joe's horse went lame, or its owner went down with bronchitis, or if anything interrupted the weekly supplies to these isolated families.

The late Mr. Harry Melling recalled such a calamity in the days of his childhood. There were no candles. In desperation, his father plaited a piece of twine, soaked it in a saucer of linseed oil, and lighted the family to the extent of about half a match power for a week !

Yet, even with all her oppressive work and constant pregnancy, the mother of those days was not spared in the struggle to eke out the family budget. Far into the evening hours she picked and boiled and potted the shrimps brought home by her husband and sons, and by early morning she was off on foot over the rut-ridden moss roads, burdened down by two baskets laden with the previous evening's work. She hawked them round the Blackpool boarding houses and hotels, and walked all the way home similarly dragged down, this time with household provisions which the proceeds had enabled her to buy in.

Not surprisingly, in those days, sand-grown lassies were bundled off into service as swiftly as maybe, to ease the overcrowding in cottage homes. And there was a great distinction in being selected for service at the Hall where often generations of the same family were employed, either in the grounds, the greenhouses, the home-farm, or in the servants' quarters.

The Squire's employees were often housed in lodges dotted about the Estate, for which they paid 1/-d. a year. Fifty years ago, Mr. William Pearson (now of Heyhouses) married Miss Jane Anyon, and moved into Shepherd's Lodge, bordering the Fairhaven Golf Course. They set up home on 16/-d. a week (later 18/-d., and finally 35/-d.). There was neither gas nor electricity at the cottage, and drinking water had to be trundled on a cart all the way from the stable yard near the Hall. Since the old pump was full of grubs, rainwater collected in tubs supplied all the other needs. Firewood from the Squire's woodyard kept the family fires blazing, and at Christmas a lump of Scotch beef came down from the Hall.

They were simple, but happy days, when employees took a pride in their work, and a keen pleasure in being of service to " The Family."

We can think of a young Carleton couple arriving here almost a century ago, swaying along the rutted lanes with all their worldly goods and a two-year-old lad packed on to a flat farm cart. Their home was to be one of the old cobble cottages (now demolished) in Commonside, Ansdell, but the young wife, who had not yet set eyes on her new home, was horrified to find the thatch infested with rats. For 26 weeks, whilst the roof was being renewed, the family took refuge in one of the whitewashed cottages near the Smithy, at Heyhouses. Soon, this couple, who were to bring forth five boys and six girls (all but one of whom survived), were engaged in a life or death struggle to succeed at farming.

The land had been sadly neglected, rabbits had over-run the fields, and,

Old Cottages, Commonside. (*Photograph by J. Salmon, Ltd., Sevenoaks*).

in a fit of malice, the outgoing tenant had hacked all the fruit trees and bushes down by the roots. This was a serious setback in times when, literally, what you did not grow you did not eat. For years every spare penny was earmarked for wiring off the rabbits.

The schoolboys of the family got up before five o'clock, milked the cows, and set off for Lytham, on foot, laden with milk kits. Milk was threepence a quart. They hawked it round the houses and hotels and often came back to breakfast with as much as they had sold. Then it was time to pick up a lunch packet and the younger children, and trudge back once more into Lytham for a day's schooling. Tea-time was also milking time again, and the boys set out once more with their heavy kits. In the evenings there was plenty of work to do, around the farm, in the vegetable plot, and the garden, and after that, presumably, the rest of the day was their own.

They made cheese too, but as the late Mr. John Rossall (the original two-year-old lad) recalled for me, years ago : " Cheese made off sandy lands will not keep, though it eats very well."

Mr. Rossall's father died, comparatively young, in the 1880's, having first earned the reputation, according to Mr. Thomas Fair, the Clifton Agent, of being : " The finest farmer on the estate.' The farm was carried on by the children under the direction of their mother whose ancestry and upbringing had fitted her for the task.

Mr. John Rossall s memories were uproarious and varied. He could tell of a little man with gold ear-rings who used to bring coal in a flat-bottomed cart and unload it near the White Church. It was taken away by horse and cart and hawked round the district at 9d. per cwt., but even at that price, and for coal of the finest quality, it took six weeks to sell one load.

He could tell of Old Blind Jonathan Martin who played the fiddle, or sometimes a harmonium on wheels in the streets of Lytham for a living, always accompanied by his dog. Blind Martin, a great composer of hymns (some of his work was acknowledged by Queen Victoria) spent his last years with his relatives at Leach Lodge farm.

Then there was old Tom Miller, a skilled carpenter of Lytham who never earned more than £1 per week though he lived long enough to walk four times to Preston Guild ; and a lusty character from Commonside who, out of sheer curiosity, walked to Preston Horse Fair and, hiccuping madly, came clattering back in the middle of the night in charge of three completely unnecessary and highly irrelevant purchases. " But what are we going to do with the things ? " enquired a demented wife from the bedroom window whilst the three great beasts clattered and thrashed about in the back yard.

" Shovvem in t'wesh-house," came back the happy reply, " and if all three weant go in, we can fotch one into th'back kitchin." (This was obviously one " sandgrown 'un " who had taken more than his usual " drop o' 'llowance ").

As a boy, Mr. Rossall remembered all the shops in Lytham being "dressed up for Christmas." " One of the butchers," to quote his own words : " told us lads to scrape and clean everything up, then go to the corn merchants and get a shop-ful of straw. Then he (the butcher) drove in two highland cattle " . . . which were kept in the shop, as an attraction, and slaughtered for Christmas beef.

He remembered " Soft Jemmy," a harmless simpleton of the district who made a point of inspecting all the new babies. Whenever he discovered a black-headed one, he smiled with pride and declared fondly : " Id's mine ! "

At one time, the Rossall family employed eight or nine Irishmen who, one evening, settled down for a session at cards with some of the locals. Among them was Big Peter, a rough giant who had been misbehaving himself, cleared out of Ireland, and came over for the potato picking. Things were going against the " sandgrown 'uns," and Big Peter was just about to put down the last card when Mr. Rossall hastily dropped his hat down over the candle and doused the light ! He also took the precaution of keeping out of Big Peter's way for three or four days, otherwise he might well have been " murthered."

The only surviving member of that original fine family is Miss Jane Rossall, M.B.E. (first woman councillor of this borough, former Mayor, ex-Alderman, retired County Magistrate, and Commandant of the Starr Hills Hospital during the first world war), and whose lifetime of distinguished service to this community was crowned in 1949 by the presentation of the Honorary Freedom of the Borough. Though in her eighties and, alas! sightless, this wonderful lady still takes a keen and zestful interest in local affairs and copes with a voluminous correspondence and a host of welcome callers.

Long after St. Annes came to birth, the Squire and his guests formed shooting parties, combing the remote sandhills of the parish in search of a good bag. Runners went on ahead to warn cottage tenants who promptly snatched up their children and locked them safely indoors until the danger was over.

Even after a long day's work, the " sandgrown 'uns " still had the capacity for enjoying themselves when occasion offered. The merest hint of a wreck sent them scurrying beachwards, and whether it was bags of peas, kitchen knives, or something in a bottle, or a cask, nothing was ever so swiftly gathered up or so neatly whipped out of sight. There was at ime, many years ago, when a cargo of hams was washed up at Ansdell. The

Commonside fishermen who turned out in force that night managed to look surprisingly innocent next morning, though many a Commonside back garden had developed strange contours during the night. When the heat cooled off, out came the hams, and local families lived like lords on this unexpected booty from the sea.

Amongst the old farming families there were some doughty card-playing characters. Often they embarked, not on a light-hearted session of whist, but on a tight-lipped contest of skill which proceeded through the night and concluded with an acrimonious post-mortem just before milking time next morning.

Similarly, the dancing " sandgrown 'uns " approached their terpsichorean activities with ponderous solemnity. Let the young lady be fair, and smart, and altogether captivating in every other way, but if her accomplishments fell short in the schottische, quadrille, lancers, or the waltz, she was not only regarded as " nowt a pound " by the dancing farmers, but told so, in as many words.

Many years ago, a well known local farmer, then a smart youth, spotted a divine young creature seated on the other side of the dance floor.

" Go on, Billy, I bet you dursen't go and ask her for a waltz," challenged one of his pals.

" I bet you I dare," replied our farmer, who promptly did just that. Unfortunately, the idol of delight proved but an indifferent performer and, after tripping up her partner once or twice, she blushingly explained that she had had an accident that day, and that a lump of iron had fallen on her foot.

" Aye ! " muttered the youth, leading her disgustedly back to her seat, " and I think oo's still theer ! "

Previous generations can remember many a night's dancing in Jameson's barn at Leach Lodge Farm, St. Annes. Candles, slivered to soap-flake thinness, were scattered on the wooden floor of the old granary. The feet of the dancers did the rest. Will Wade from Mad Nook on the Moss played the accompaniment on his violin, and as Miss Margaret Jameson recalled

Dance Hall of bye-gone days. Barn at Leach Lodge Farm.

for me recently: " He could nearly make it talk. He had had lessons, at 1/-d. a time, and when he drew that bow across the strings, his arm waved as gracefully as a swan." There was also an accordianist, and sometimes, though it was not very popular, a tin whistle.

On Mondays, Wednesdays and Fridays, the late John Jameson acted as Master of Ceremonies, lit the powerful paraffin lamp hanging down from the roof, and segregated his dancers on forms at opposite ends of the barn. A farmer all his life, yet when it came to dancing, John Jameson, who was a big man, was " as light as a feather on his feet and could dance all night with a book on his head." By all accounts, he ran everything " very strict and decorous," but the " sandgrown 'uns " had an irrepressible sense of fun. One of the veterans who still remembers the old barn dances recalled that entrance to the barn loft was effected by way of wooden, open-backed stairs.

" Course, being proper little gentlemen, like," says he with a sly chuckle, " we allus stood back an' let th'ladies go up t'fost ! "

Now, the dancing, and the music have fallen away into the past, and never again will the farm-lad, constricted in his unfamiliar collar, but suprisingly light on his feet, come clumping across from his form to the lady of his choice and ask gravely : " Art ockapied ? Well, if tha's a mind, ah'll ockapy thee." These were the days when man made his own simple pleasures, and Plain Jane often triumphed over her prettier rival.

Leach Lodge Farm.

Leach Lodge Farm belongs now to Mr. R. F. Williamson, a builder, who has done a great deal of reconstruction work on the old place. Leach Lodge too was found to be a cottage within a house, with cobble walls, and hand-made, and mass-produced bricks, all welded together to make a home of the future out of a farmhouse steeped in memories of the past.

THE LIVELIEST INN IN THE PARISH

On the 19th September, 1826, Thomas Greaves, by acknowledging his indebtedness to our Sovereign Lord the King in the sum of Thirty Pounds, was granted a licence for the selling of ale, beer, and other liquors, at premises known as the Trawl Boat at Lytham. (But then, the hamlet of Heyhouses had always been included within that ancient parish).

The suppression of all manner of gaming, whether by " cards, draughts or dice," the prohibition from the premises of " bull or bear-baiting and cockfighting," and the discouragement of drunkenness, tippling, and the company of " men or women of notoriously bad fame, or dissolute boys

The Trawl Boat Inn, showing Mrs. Mary Houseman, the last licensee (second from left).
(*By kind permission of the Scott family*).

and girls " were all conditions which marched hand in hand with the concession. The worthy Innkeeper was further bidden to maintain " good rule and order " and decent hours.

Having regard to the conditions of the times it would seem that a weighty burden had been placed upon the shoulders of Mine Host at the Trawl Boat, though in one respect the law was more leniently disposed than it is today. Licensing hours had not been thought of, and liquor could be sold at any hour of the day or night, except " during the usual hours of divine service on Sundays."

These were the vigorous days of Lytham's early prosperity. Trim schooners plied the river. The lumbering stage-coach rattled to a halt by the fish-stones. And whilst the segregated sea-bathers enjoyed the salt water " as well internally as externally," the Lytham natives earned for themselves a solid reputation as an elbow-raising community. Even so, they were said to have averaged upwards of 80 years of age " unless hard drinking laid them untimely beneath the sod," and long before the time of Thomas Greaves the thirsty of the parish were wont to converge upon the Trawl Boat.

Then it was one of the typical cobble-and-thatch buildings to be found in profusion, at that time, in the Fylde. Nevertheless, it succeeded in attracting the summer visitors from Lytham, and in' 1822 one of them contributed a piece to " The Babbler " describing the attractions and diversions offered by the district, and suggesting, amongst other things, that " one may even trip to the Hay- Houses and get bad ale."

During the 1860's, the present imposing building replaced its humble white-washed predecessor. Towering above neighbouring white cottages, and solidly guarding the cross roads, the new brick Trawl Boat renewed and expanded its influence and once more became the hub and centre of village life.

Thither gravitated visiting gentlemen to indulge in a rustic tipple whilst the ladies strolled round the inn gardens and enjoyed a milder beverage on the lawn. Many, before leaving, would acquaint themselves with the landlord's pig housed in a cobble building out in the yard ; and a bowling green was laid out, as the century wore on, for the entertainment of guests.

All the year round, and non-stop, the good cheer to be found at the Trawl Boat was the magnet that lured the inhabitants like so many needles, often to the exclusion of all thoughts of work ! On Sundays, this mecca of the thirsty reared up like a beckoning angel half way along the dusty track leading to St. Cuthbert's Church at Lytham, and many an otherwise well-intentioned churchgoer fell by the wayside and, by some strange chance, found himself claiming his accustomed corner of The Snug.

Eventually, Lady Eleanor Cecily Clifton became greatly troubled about the remoter parishioners and sought to combat the counter-attraction by providing afternoon services in the Old Heyhouses Schoolhouse. In 1873 the Chapel of Ease dedicated to St. Anne was built, but the inn's popularity declined not a tittle.

Indeed, the whole history of this lively inn bristles with colourful anecdote. There brawny men wagered their strength in the carrying of flagstones over

White cottages and Smithy (extreme left). (*Photograph by Frank Dean, Esq.*).

a pint of ale, and fights broke out, checking the laughter and song, and adjourning, as like as not, to the well-worn cobble yard where the ancient pump saw many a good old-fashioned rough-and-tumble.

Many of our old ones could remember the wheelwright's shop standing idle, and the blacksmith's anvil lying silent, whilst the two neighbours dallied away long happy hours on the other side of the cross roads. Anyone requiring their services had first to lure the thirsty pair out of the saloon bar.

Many of the farming fraternity were too intent upon the Trawl Boat, so it was said, to pay sufficient heed to their crops. The land fell into neglect, rents relapsed into arrears, and local fishermen who drew their harvest from the sea were becoming increasingly inclined to push the boat out a mile inland !

Wives and families suffered as the standard of work declined, and to this day, at " The Elms " in Heyhouses, there is a hedge which ought to have followed a straight line but which, probably due to the proximity of the Trawl Boat, and frequent attacks of thirst, finished up pursuing a dog's-leg course.

In 1866 Thomas Bennett became the landlord of the " Troul Boat," and he was followed by Mary Houseman whose faded memory, until recent years, still lingered with a few old " sandgrown 'uns." Mrs. Houseman and her family kept the inn and farmed a few acres, and did a roaring trade, especially on Lytham Club Day. On this occasion of local rejoicing, Lytham's cab proprietors maintained a non-stop lightning shuttle-service to Heyhouses, unloading the thirsty gentlemen at the Trawl Boat, and hauling the full ones back. Fortunately, on the occasion of this mild annual debauch, the constabulary was disposed to wink a benevolently indulgent eye so long as the merrymaker, no matter at what perilous angle, could still stand on his own two feet. Any prostrate upon the ground, of course, were promptly run in !

Jests and practical jokes were all part of the tradition, and there is a lovely story of the man who walked home from Warton carrying a young piglet in a sack slung over his shoulder. By Heyhouses, his throat was as parched as the desert sands and, resting his burden down at the Trawl Boat, he set about alleviating his sufferings before weaving a zig-zag course for home. When he untied the sack, to his wife's fury and his own fuddled astonishment, there emerged a black dog ! " Was a pi-ig, then a do-og ! " . . . this catch-phrase, chanted by local children, haunted the rest of his life and prompted many a chase.

Boardman's Farm, Regent Avenue, before the " thacking " disappeared. (*From a water colour by the late Walter Eastwood, reproduced by kind permission of Norman Stirrup, Esq., A.R.I.B.A., Chartered Architect*).

73

" Aye, they used to get on the spree instead of minding their waark ! " remembered the old ones. Fortunately or otherwise, the problem resolved itself when, on one doomful day, probably in the early 'eighties, a brawl broke out and spilled over noisily on to the steps of the Trawl Boat just as Lady Drummond, the mother of our late Squire, happened to be driving past in her carriage. It was mid-day. All honest men should have been decently about their business. The lady was shocked to the core.

Shortly after, whether by her intervention or not, the licence was withdrawn, and the inn's career came to an abrupt and decisive end. The sign was hauled down from its customary place above the front door ; flagstones were carted off to a neighbouring farm ; the cellar was filled in with earth, the bar became a kitchen, and The Snug was turned into a parlour.

Over rooms once heavy with ale fumes and gusty good cheer now stole the gentler fragrance of coffee, the tinkle of silver on china, and the muted chatter of abstemious society. An aura of respectability had descended upon this riotous old inn, and many were the hearts that were sad. " It should never have been closed," some said. Others, with equal fervour declared . . . " It should never have been opened ! "

Only the photograph remains of the old alehouse days, and perhaps a " feeling " that still one gets . . . and stubborn circles worn into an upstairs floor by the cheeses of long, long ago.

AN OLD COUNTRY CRAFT

In a few rural communities up and down the country one can still run to earth some of the now comparatively rare makers of Corn Dollies. This parish has one. Mr. Bob Scott, whose family live at the Trawl Boat, lives across the road in one of the whitewashed cottages at Heyhouses. The neatness and artistry of his creations must surely place him in the front ranks of all the Corn Dolly men of Great Britain.

For a few weeks at harvest time each year, Mr. Scott revives this pre-Christian craft which stemmed originally from the pagan custom of offering an appeasement or supplication to the gods of harvest and seed-time. The folk of centuries ago believed that the spirit of the corn could be captured and preserved in the last sheaf cut from the fields. Often it was crudely fashioned into a female effigy and carried amidst solemn rites to the seasonal festival. During the winter months it was carefully preserved in the farmhouse to ensure the continuance of the crops.

These pagan rituals were not discouraged by the establishment of the Christian Church, but were woven, along with other old customs, such as Beating the Bounds and Loaf-Mass, into the pattern of church and village life.

In scattered parts of the country it is still possible to watch the Corn Dolly, sometimes dressed in woman's clothes and crowned with a wreath of flowers, being carried by a procession of villagers to the Mell or Harvest Supper. Much of the old superstition has long died away, but the custom persists, and there are infinite regional variations.

Scotland and Northumberland call it the Kern Baby, or Kirn Baba. In Wales it is The Hag ; in Germany the Corn Mother, or Grandmother ;

Bob Scott, with a selection of Corn Dollies. Note the old pump (at rear of the Trawl Boat).
(*Photograph by Alderman A. F. Williamson, C.C.*).

Southern counties call it The Nack ; and in other parts it makes an annual appearance under the name of The Mare, or The Queen.

Unlike most Corn Dolly artists, Mr. Scott's gift was not handed down by generations of ancestors. It is obvious, however, that his forebears were richly endowed with the various skills of true countrymen. Farming, stock raising, thatching, but perhaps best of all, gardening and horticulture, were and still are second nature to the Scotts.

Years ago, Bob's father, the late Mr. Ralph Scott, used to weave a five-strand ribbon of corn straw to wear round his hat during harvest. The idea of fashioning something more elaborate from the green stems began to germinate in the imagination of his son. Bob, a farmer born and bred, could judge to a nicety when the corn was best ready to be worked. An illustrated book borrowed from the library gave him the first inkling of how to begin. From that small beginning has emerged the bold and imaginative skill which every season produces a crop of beautiful designs.

Bells, lanterns, angel dolls and tassels, make a regular appearance, and living only a good stretch of the legs from Lytham, it is not surprising to find a variety of windmills. Ambitious chandelier arrangements, some having up to eight arms and pendants, are slung in profusion from the cottage ceiling. An exquisite miniature corn stack goes regularly to Church at harvest time. And, as might be expected from a countryman with the scent of the sea in his nostrils, there is always an anchor to be found amongst the collection.

Samples of this lovely work have been exhibited at the Royal Lancashire

Show and despatched all over the world, and now that this delicate and ancient craft has been revived within the community, steps have been taken to ensure that it continues on into the future. David Scott, a fresh-faced young giant, has been leaning over his father's shoulder and picking up a hint or two. One day, perhaps, with much practice, he too may attain to the skill of his comely father whose dexterity has been demonstrated to television audiences more than once in recent times.

"SAMFIRTH"—THE POOR MAN'S ASPARAGUS

Not long ago, in a neighbouring village, there was a sale of work in full swing. Jams and chutneys were being snapped up in quick style. Nobody, however, was brave enough to bid for a pound jar of some strange concoction, wearing a weird sounding name, until a chance memory prompted one lady to buy it and present it to the Jameson family, now living in Marton Moss, but for long years the tenants of Leach Lodge Farm, St. Annes. There, the delicacy was greatly appreciated, and to quote their own words, " it didn't reign so long ! "

The Jameson family, and all the old timers of the district, were well acquainted with this fleshy perennial weed which was found in profusion amongst the marshes around Guide's House at Warton. One regular July chore was to take the horse and cart and gather in sufficient supplies of this glabrous, stout-stemmed and succulent herb to keep the household in pickles through the year.

Samphire, or Crithmum Maritimum, is a curious marine plant which grows along coasts from Britain southwards, along the Mediterranean, and even as far as the Black Sea. Its name, meaning the herb of St. Peter, is a corruption of the Italian, San Pietro, but the " sandgrown 'uns " called it " Samfirth." Many a 7-lb. jar of this spicy, salty pickle enlivened the plain fare of the old families, but it seems that the present generation " won't be bothered."

The stems, woody at the base, were first given a good washing, boiled in water, strained dry, cut off in little twigs, and pickled in spiced vinegar. It was eaten, held betwixt thumb and finger, and run sideways through the teeth, and those who know it will tell you that it is delicious.

The seeds of the samphire are borne along water gullies and deposited on salty marshland where they take root. The samphire prefers solitude. When other seeds are arrested by, and begin to grow about, its roots, it moves on, leaving vague trails of green vegetation in its wake, and we can watch this botannical drama unfolding on Lytham's beach. Within a handful of years the samphire, which often settles around coastal rocks and must find our shingle very much to its taste, has travelled along from near the Bakery and reached the site of the old pier.

Some may like to try their hand at this genuine " sand-grown " pickle, in which case there is another, slightly more exotic, recipe which can be used. Wash the samphire thoroughly, place in a jar with pepper corns and shavings of horseradish ; cover them with a boiling mixture of vinegar and dry cider (light wine or water) in equal parts and salt. Place in oven for one hour to infuse. Seal, and store.

Do take care to identify the samphire correctly, and remember that it is best harvested, according to the authorities, in July.

ST. ANNES ROAD WEST, ST. ANNES-ON-SEA.

61682 (JV)

St. Annes Square showing the flower beds, each with its vase and urn, bounded by trellis work. It is notable that there is not a single motor car in sight, so the photograph was probably taken around 1900 for Valentine & Co. for use as a postcard.

THE SQUARE AND CRESCENT, ST. ANNES-ON-SEA.

222755 JV.

A 1920s scene, after buses had been introduced in 1923. The forecourt gardens show the gardens bounded by privet hedges. On the left is Bradley & Co., fancy goods dealers, now occupied by Woolworths. The shop on the extreme right is Seymour Mead's, one of a chain of a Manchester grocery empire.

THE PARISH CHURCH OF ST. ANNE

Without resort to old maps, it is almost impossible to believe how the St. Anne's portion of the old manor of Lytham has developed during the past hundred years.

In the first half of Victoria's reign, every traveller was impressed by the uniform green flatness stretching out before him on the road to Blackpool. Along the coast lay an unbroken stretch of untamed sand-dunes. The country road, leading through the sleepy hamlet of Heyhouses, wound its way through acres of farmland. The Trawl Boat was there, with its neighbouring cluster of white cottages and a faint stirring of life. But from that point on the traveller would see but few isolated farms and small dwellings. Nothing pointed to the emergence, within half a lifetime, of a new town which one day would sweep over field and pasture and reach out to embrace Lytham itself.

The folk at that time were all parishioners of Lytham, the parish of which extended to Division Lane. Farmers and those who worked on their farms, fishermen, gamekeepers and the like, made up the tiny population.

Their church, when they cared to stretch their legs over several miles, was St. Cuthbert's at Lytham. Unfortunately for their spiritual inclinations, the Trawl Boat reared up before then, half way along the route, and this counter-attraction, and the distance, inspired Lady Eleanor Cecily Clifton to build a Chapel of Ease to serve the community in the undeveloped portion of the manor.

Col. Clifton, her husband, generously donated a triangular site covering two and a half acres. Lady Eleanor Cecily provided the money. The Estate supplied the bricks on the stipulation that every able-bodied man in the district should put in one day, or two half days' work with horse and cart, bringing them from the kiln to the site.

The kiln was at Marton Moss behind the (now demolished) Fold Row which stood beside the old " Shovels Inn." When the bricks were ready there was keen competition between local farmers whose natural zest was spurred on by the promise of £1 in prize money to the one tipping the first load on the site.

Rivalry ran amok as the laden milk floats and marl carts lumbered unsteadily across the badly rutted moss roads. Some never made the distance but were tumbled ignominiously off the highway by more energetic competitors. Up Mellings Lane, into School Lane (St. Annes Road East), past Daddy Whiteside's farm (Beauclerk Gardens) they rumbled, the forerunners so closely matched that in the end three " sandgrown 'uns " sportingly helped tip the winning load and shared the coveted prize.

The foundation stone was laid in 1872, and the church, built towerless, plainly, in Queen Anne style, and costing over £4,000, was completed in 1873. Despite all the physical support for the scheme, not everyone was enamoured of the site of the graveyard, and some of the old local diehards declared frankly that they had no fancy for being " scrat up be th'rapputs ! "

In August 1873 the church was dedicated to St. Anne in memory of Lady Anne Bentinck, an aunt of Lady Eleanor Cecily. It was St. Anne's Church, and it was on the sea, and two years later, when Elijah Hargreaves and his associates launched the new town, custom and usage had already manufactured the name.

In 1875 the first interment took place, that of two-year-old George Melling from Mellings Lane. The child pulled a kettle of boiling water from the

The Parish Church about 1880, taken from corner of Beauclerk Gardens, and showing the lych gate on corner of St. Annes Road East and Church Road. This lych gate was later transferred to its present location. (*From a photograph kindly loaned by the Vicar, Rev. E. S. Pickup, M.A.*).

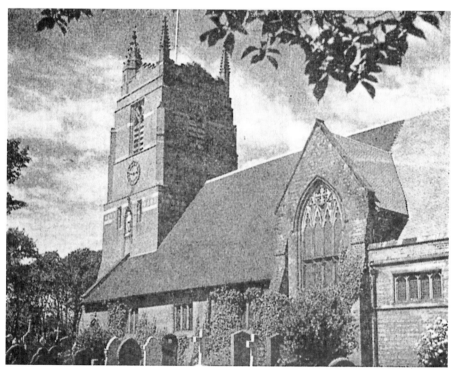

The Church as it is today. (*Photograph by Alderman A. F. Williamson, C.C.*).

hob and he was scalded to death, and this tragic event evoked yet another act of compassionate charity from the Lady of the Manor. She erected the headstone, which stands on the right hand side of the path a few yards from the church door. By harsh coincidence, another infant brother, also named George, was soon to follow the first Melling child into the same grave.

Nowadays, perhaps, it is not easy to create a mental picture of the church in its original form. Then it had the newly minted look of a recent erection. No ivy clung about its walls, and the bricks had not mellowed with time. It had a small steeple in place of the familiar tower of today. The tower was added only in 1890, and again the revered Patroness came forward with the gift of bells. There were no trees then to give shade and quiet to this piece of hallowed ground, and only gradually did the headstones begin to punctuate the unbroken green.

Since those early days many notable gifts have enhanced the beauty of St. Anne's Parish Church. The organ, originally given by Lady Eleanor Cecily, was rebuilt in 1934 at considerable cost. There are some fine stained glass memorial windows ; a handsome carved reredos of Caen stone, presented by the tenants in 1881 in memory of Thomas Henry (" Harry ") Clifton, Lady Eleanor Cecily's only son who died tragically in the prime of his life ; the Queen Victoria Jubilee memorial clock, which one old resident remembers standing on a stone pedestal just outside St. Anne's Station until the rumbling of the trains and carriers' carts upset its mechanism, when it was transferred to the church in 1899 . . . during which year many of the trees were planted.

More recent additions include the beautiful panelling in the sanctuary, the bishop's throne, the children's corner, the lectern which takes the form of a bronze eagle, and the pulpit.

The north aisle, vestry, lady chapel and choir vestry, have all been added since the original building, and the baptistry, annexed to the west end in 1920 deserves a special mention. It cost £1,600, and has been described " an architectural gem."

ST. ANNES

AN OPAL FROM THE SAND

The story of the town of St. Annes, though recent, is as romantic as any pioneering saga of the western prairies. During the second half of the last century Lytham was well established as a seaside resort, and Blackpool enjoyed a similar popularity.

At the western end of Lytham's ancient parish, however, still lay vast tracts of undeveloped field-lands, acres of untamed sand, and a long unbroken stretch of desolate foreshore.

The few inhabitants, whose tiny white homes blazed out brilliantly from a backcloth of green, were so far outnumbered by teeming hordes of rabbits that it was said to be impossible to set a foot down without disturbing one of their congregations.

It was a wild place, and windswept, where larks soared up in their hundreds and filled the sky with sweet music. There grew the spiky starr grass, lush blue-berries, evening primroses, heartsease, wild orchid, and many a rare species which building activities had pushed from other parts of the coast.

On a high sand-bank (now Lightburne Avenue) the wooden lighthouse, (successor to the first stone one which stood on Lytham's beach until it fell in a gale in January, 1863) flashed out its message to mariners in the Estuary. A stonesthrow away two cottages (near corner of Riley Avenue and Clifton Drive) housed the lighthouse-keeper and one of the Clifton game-keepers.

Built over as the town is now, it is difficult to picture what it must have looked like a hundred years ago. The rough track that was Common Lane (Church Road) linked up, then as now, with Headroomgate Road, and its long stretch towards Ansdell was punctuated by seven small homesteads, nestling beside the lane and turning their faces to the sea. School Lane (St. Anne's Road East) boasted not a single cottage, but along Headroomgate Road, just past the Vicarage, there was Ryeheys Farm, and further still, Greaves' old farm and another ancient cottage standing on what were to become the corners of Ashley Road.

Headroomgate Farm still stands on the opposite side of the road, and adjoining, up Twiggy Lane (Highbury Road East) were its two tiny tied cottages. Further up Twiggy Lane was Twiggy Hill Farm.

Along High Dam Lane (Kilnhouse Lane) there were four farmsteads and this area was known locally as " The West End." Much nearer the sea was the small hamlet of Cross Slack.

Heyhouses Lane was by far the most populous portion of the parish's extremity. Apart from a few miniature homes, there were a number of important and old-established farms ranked on both sides of the lane. With the occasional rumbling of carts and carriages, and the tranquil passing of cattle, Heyhouses Lane, in contrast to some of the deserted tracks, must have seemed like one of the great highways of the world.

Certainly there was nothing about the district at that time to set the world on fire. True enough, from 1863 a single line railway linked Lytham with Blackpool, and in 1872 Col. Clifton laid down to the Blackpool boundary The Drive which took his name. But no-one had yet formulated any plans for the building of another new town or, if they had thought about it, had done nothing about putting them into action. Mr. James Fair, the one-time Clifton Agent, had cherished the notion of wresting a Utopia from the sand, but the ambition died with the man and it was left to others to set things in motion.

In the summer of 1874, Mr. Elijah Hargreaves, a full-faced bustling Lancastrian business man from the Rossendale Valley, happened to be taking

View from top of railway bridge in 1885, showing houses in St. David's Road South and St. Annes Road East.

St. Annes Road West (The Square) in 1885, looking seaward. Garden Street on right. Rear of Montauban Chambers on extreme left.

a holiday in Blackpool. A fine day took him strolling along the beach in the direction of Lytham, but long before he reached that town his instincts had sharpened to the possibilities of developing this huge unspoiled plot and building a seaside resort which might far out-rank all the others along the Estuary of the Ribble. Southport, for instance, might be thought by some to be too relaxing ; Blackpool, with its exposed position, was at times undeniably bleak ; and Lytham . . . well, it was Lytham !

Here, however, was a ready-made site for the building of something quite different. A grand town, a planned town, with wide roads and elegant houses, ample gardens and generous parks. The sandy sub-soil was perfect, the westerly breezes were laden with good health, and now that the railway was established, what Lancashire business man would not take advantage of parking his family on the coast and scuttling over to join them when the demands of commerce allowed ?

So ran the thoughts of Elijah Hargreaves whose polished boots eventually creaked into Lytham and deposited their owner on the doorstep of the Clifton Estate Office. A productive conversation sprang up between the man from the Rossendale Valley and Mr. Thomas (son of James) Fair, J.P. This second Mr. Fair had inherited all the enthusiasm of his father for a

First Lytham Lighthouse (destroyed by gales 1863) which stood on beach opposite Lord Ashton's bungalow.

82

town-building scheme. The Clifton family in general was sympathetic to the project, and a Mr. Maxwell, of Messrs. Maxwell & Tuke, Architects of Blackpool Tower, had already spoken in glowing terms of such a proposal.

Later that year (1874) the St. Annes Land and Building Company was formed, taking its name from the Chapel of Ease which had been built the previous year. The Company, consisting of eight Rossendale businessmen, including Elijah Hargreaves, was registered on 14th October, and started off with a lease on a square mile of land upon which they had agreed to expend £70,000 on developments within a few years.

This bold, decisive, and idealistic action on the part of the eight pioneers was to lead them into all manner of difficulties before the new town was launched. First of all, people declined " to lock up their money for their grandchildren," and then again, there was an acute shortage of accommodation for the hundreds of workmen who would be required.

Eventually, two contracts were let, one for the Promenade (Messrs. Taylor & Duckworth), and the other for the St. Annes Hotel, shared between Messrs. Ogden, Hamilton, Roberts, Walmsley and others.

It was 2nd February, 1875, before the inaugural sod was cut, the craftsmen were set to work, and the first thin wails of the infant town drifted out over the sandy wastes.

Soon, the first batch of workmen became discouraged, drifted away, and had to be replaced. Wooden huts were provided to house them where they slept on the trestle tables by night and ate their meals from them by day. One enterprising character, by name of Davenport, opened a western-style log cabin store and did a lively trade, and a branch line, laid down what was to become The Square, brought piles of bricks, timber and other materials, until the whole place was choked almost to a standstill.

Two pairs of semis were to be built in St. Andrew's Road South to accommodate workmen, and twelve more in Common Lane (Church Road) for the same purpose.

First of all there was the important stone-laying ceremony, and the one chosen to perform it was our late Squire, Mr. John Talbot Clifton, then a seven-year-old schoolboy. In laying the foundation stone of the hotel, on 31st March, 1875, young Master Clifton was at the same time launching a whole new town.

Once again, the capacity of the " sandgrown 'uns " for letting their hair down and celebrating all local events in fullest measure was colourfully exhibited in the scenes which attended the ceremony. A special train brought the well-wishers through from Lytham to the little level crossing at St. Annes. In front of the small wooden shed which served as a station, a platform had been erected, with a banner fluttering the message : " Success to St. Annes."

Amongst the excited crowds, members of the Clifton family, Lord Winmarleigh, Mayors from all over the county, and many of the nobility and gentry, assembled to give the new town a good send-off. More than 100 guests responded to the toast : " Success to the town of St. Annes," at a luncheon provided at the Clifton Arms Hotel by Lady Eleanor Cecily Clifton. Lancashire newspapers echoed the sentiments and gave wide publicity to the new town, which had taken its name from the church, but which was soon to become widely famed as " The Opal of the West."

Despite the initial excitement, however, disillusion was soon in danger of setting in. The early shareholders lost a great deal of their money. The early workmen often lost heart. Only the grim determination of the founders kept the ship afloat during the early years of disheartening slump.

Fortunately the scheme had attracted such sturdy characters as Mr. W. J. Porritt, an inspired builder who turned a blind eye on adversity, sunk nearly a quarter of a million pounds into the new town, and left behind a host of gracious stone houses as a perpetual monument to his unique brand of courage and foresight.

For three years St. Annes remained within the jurisdiction of the Lytham authority, but in 1878 it was created a separate district with government over 8,028 acres. Its Gas Company had been registered in 1875.

In 1885 the Company were able to throw their newly built pier open to the public. Three churches were established during the 'nineties ; the Roman Catholic Church in 1891 ; the Drive Wesleyan Methodist in 1892 ; and the Congregational in 1896.

Gas motor trams operated between St. Annes and South Shore in 1897 but were sold out and electrified in 1898. Meantime, as the result of an Act of Parliament in 1895, the South Promenade was beginning to emerge.

In 1895 too, the Local Government Board became the St. Annes Urban District Council which was served by enterprising men with great ambitions for " The Opal of the West." Immediately before the First World War, the Council were intent on building an open air swimming bath, and acquiring St. George's Gardens for the town. For long years the question of the Gardens (which had been privately owned and had lost money, and parts of which were either derelict, rented by Cartmells' Nurseries, or let off as playing fields to private schools), had severed the ratepayers into two warring camps. All were unanimous in wanting the Gardens for the town, but many had a strong aversion to paying for them. Lively meetings were held, both in support of, and in opposition to, the scheme for purchasing the plot, and there were hot words and high feelings within the town when, on the eve of the poll which had been demanded by the residents, Lord Ashton stepped in with a dramatic announcement of his intention to buy the Gardens and give them to St. Annes.

Lord Ashton was a linoleum manufacturer from Lancaster. He had spent many holidays on our coast, taken an interest in golf, and formed an affection for the town. His Lordship had been kept in close touch with all the machinations attendant upon the Gardens Scheme, but his generous intentions, revealed at " Ryelands," Lancaster, to the late Councillor J. H. Taylor, then Chairman of the Board, were rendered all the more dramatic by a curious atmosphere of cloak-and-dagger secrecy.

When the news broke forth, the people of the town rejoiced, and the gift, which originally cost Lord Ashton £21,350, was extended by another £4,526 for the purchase of an extra plot. Thereafter the Gardens were developed for the benefit, and to the increased attraction, of the town, and became known by the name of their open-handed donor.

Nor did Lord Ashton's bequests stop there. He paid out £10,000 for the War Memorial, and the St. Annes War Memorial Hospital could not have opened on Charter Day, 1922, without gifts amounting to £20,000 from the same warm-hearted source.

Thus and thus, with high ideals, immense courage, and constant triumph over difficulties, the little town of St. Annes got away to a promising start. There were many things yet to be accomplished which could only be achieved with time, and with the same brand of visionary zeal which prompted Elijah Hargreaves (who died in 1904) to seek out men of faith and inspire them to build the town that will remember them forever.

The first rated house in St. Annes. Wooden bungalow occupied by Mr. and Mrs. John Heap, (1875). (*Picture kindly loaned by the Heap family*).

THE EARLY DAYS OF A NEW TOWN

In February, 1875, the inaugural sod was cut for the building of St. Annes. On 31st March of that year, the foundation stone was laid at the hotel. Several weeks before either of these events, a Rossendale couple were set down by train beside a platelayer's cabin (St. Annes Station), and left to grope their way through a wilderness of sand.

"I shan't be able to exist here," declared the lady emphatically, but erroneously, as it turned out, for the Heap family had the intense pleasure of watching St. Annes growing up all around them during the next fifty years.

In January 1875, however, all that could be seen, apart from the railway line and the occasional white splash of a building in the distance, was the wooden lighthouse perched high on a sand-bank and with its two white cottages squatting in the folds of the dunes.

The couple's new home (the first rated house in St. Annes), was a small wooden bungalow set immediately east of the railway between Springfield Road and Hove Road. Their furniture was brought in a railway wagon which was uncoupled outside the front door and left for two hours until the contents had been removed. The engine came back later to draw away the empty wagon !

About the same time another early settler arrived in the district, at the age of 20, with a horse and cart and building materials, from Bury. The horse was stabled at a Headroomgate Road farm. Its

Second Lytham Lighthouse, wooden structure which functioned until 1901, being located on sandhill (now Lightburne Avenue).

owner took refuge with Mrs. Cartmell, the lighthouse-keeper's wife. Next morning, when he looked out on an endless expanse of sand, he said, " I was quite ready for going back ! " Yet he stayed . . . and it would seem that the early pioneers, many of whom arrived against their own wishes, sooner or later became caught up in the challenge and excitement of building the new health resort. They had stumbled uninvited upon a way of life centred upon honest toil, simple pleasures, and wide open spaces, and the sea and boats and fishing, and building and squabbling, somehow stole into their blood.

If comparatively few were present at the stone-laying ceremony, others were soon coming in droves to be in on the new scheme. Two houses were being rushed up in St. Andrew's Road South. " Alpha House " became the first Post Office. Mr. Clement Rawstron of Rossendale was appointed Postmaster, and his son, Mr. William Rawstron, was sworn in by Mr. Thomas Fair, J.P., as the first postman.

The Rawstron family did a lively trade in the early months serving mid-day meals to as many of the 200 workmen as could push their way in before the supplies ran out, and in the evenings special trains ran some of the gangs back to their lodgings in Lytham or Blackpool, whilst others camped out rough in wooden huts.

Divine confusion reigned for many a long month. Building materials were strewn in heaps, and in wet weather the roughly made roads became quagmires of mud. A passenger train from Buxton rolled in with a wagon load of lime tacked on behind. The wagon had to be unloaded by degrees and shunted back and forth from Lytham as the railway line was required.

Apart from the stately houses of Hydro Terrace (now the principal shops in The Square), private residences were going up in St. Annes Road East (west of the church), Eastbank Road, the Promenade and Clifton Drive. Boarding and apartment houses in Wood Street and surrounding roads were beginning to appear, though West Crescent was still a hollow, and Park Road a field where the young played football.

Apart from the St. Anne's Church there were no facilities for worship until the Lytham Congregational Minister and the Rev. James Wayman of Blackpool opened a mission for the use of the Free Churches. " The Methodists, Baptists and Congregationalists, worshipped together, and supplies from the three denominations were regularly sent according to plan," recorded the Rev. J. Wayman, but the room . . . " was over a stable, and on a hot sultry day . . . ! " This joint mission stood amongst the sandy wastes of the Wood Street area.

Strangely enough, a number of high-class private schools sprang up almost overnight in the new little town. Miss Davidson's Ladies' Academy on the South Promenade, St. Anne's College (now at Windermere), Montauban School, and a host of others, drew boarding pupils from distant parts of the country.

Along with all the other worthy pioneers whose early efforts launched the town, there burst upon St. Annes, in 1875, one whose activities were to range far beyond the establishment in that year of Kilgrimol Boarding and Day School for Boys (now the District Club, Clifton Drive).

From the outset, Mr. John Allen, lately come from Preston, threw himself with tempestuous energy into the affairs of the place. He was appointed to the first Local Board, was President of the Ratepayers' Union, and he inspired the foundation of the first Working Men's Club. The first settlers must not be allowed to relapse into apathy and boredom but must be whipped (by Mr. John Allen) into feverish social and cultural activities,

St. Annes'

ON-THE-SEA

MISCELLANY

AND

ADVERTISER.

PUBLISHED   MONTHLY.

No. 1.   AUGUST.   1877.

FIRST YEAR OF PUBLICATION.

The Miscellany will be punctually delivered in St. Annes for twelve months, on prepayment of One Shilling ; or sent per post to any address on prepayment of One Shilling and Sixpence.

Communications should be addressed to the " St. Annes' Miscellany," St. Annes-on-the-Sea.

ONE PENNY,

including singing classes, musical treats, outings, and all the rest of it.

When not so engaged, this volatile town-builder was busy launching the first news-sheet. *The Miscellany* first appeared, monthly, price 1d., in 1877, and seems to have been used jointly as an advertising medium for private apartments and a vehicle for the founder's somewhat ponderous wit and forthright comment upon local affairs. The publication died a natural death within a few years, but meantime there were many other problems awaiting solution.

Firstly, the town had no fire-fighting unit and relied on messages being relayed to Blackpool whose horse-drawn brigade, after being lashed to a lather along Clifton Drive, invariably arrived in time to comment sympathetically over a heap of smoking ruins. In that manner a house on South Promenade was razed to the ground and was still smouldering two days after the outbreak.

Something had to be done to equip St. Annes with a separate service, and the first, a volunteer unit, was organised by Mr. John Allen. Even so, according to his old servant . . .

"The fire service was very primitive. The engine was kept in the Town's Yard, St. Andrew's Road North (now firemen's cottages occupy the site). The horse was sent from Whitesides', Park Road, and the firemen had to run from their places of employment as soon as the fire alarm " . . . (an old bell salvaged from a shipwreck) . . . "was given, one a postman, another a slater, a painter, and a few window cleaners. Talk about Fred Carno's Fire Brigade, natives always laughed at the turn-out."

After the "Mexico" disaster (1886), John Allen invented a "non-capsizable" lifeboat propelled by two sets of rotating paddle blades, and operated manually by five crank-handles on each side of the vessel. The blades were accommodated in the centre of the craft under a paddle-box. There were twin emergency sails and an ingenious steering device, but when eight or nine local fishermen embarked with the inventor for a trial cruise on the Ribble the "non-capsizable" lifeboat turned turtle, and a congregation of blue-jerseyed spectators almost rolled down the sand-dunes with laughing.

Mrs. Allen, who was lame, used to be a familiar figure riding through The Square in a governess cart drawn by a small pony called Bob, and her husband, who was rarely seen without his two great St. Bernard dogs, Juno and Malko, at his heels, was an equally familiar figure, striding about the sandy streets of a growing town.

After the death of his wife, Mr. Allen relinquished the school and lived for a time at "Kilgrimol Cottage," St. Annes Road East (next to Beauclerk Gardens). His stormy career came to an abrupt end in 1904 at the herbalist's shop which he had been running in Park Road.

"A man so various, born to contrariness" . . . this was perhaps a fitting epitaph, not only to John Allen, but to the many ordinary, and extraordinary characters, who came from points far afield and who, from the clash of personalities, and the conflict of ideas, clawed a beautiful town out of a wilderness of sand.

ST. ANNES PIER

The early years of the St. Annes Land and Building Company were fraught with so many difficulties and setbacks that even such steely characters as its Directors could have been forgiven for packing up in disgust and going back home to the Rossendale Valley.

Instead, they were impelled forward by a deepening sense of purpose and, as a measure of their faith, and having met during the first twelve months at the Queen's Hotel, Rawtenstall, they transferred the Company's offices to St. Annes in 1876.

By 1879, whilst financially their affairs were going from bad to worse, they decided to set about building their new pier. On 15th June, 1885, the Hon. Fred Stanley came over to perform the opening ceremony.

The New St. Annes Pier, opened 1885.

It was a narrow, modest structure, uncovered, without any imposing entrance, and boasting only a single shelter at the furthest end. On opening day, flags fluttered, steamers from Blackpool cruised by, gaily rigged, hundreds of interested spectators crowded the decking, and the lifeboat "Laura Janet," doomed to tragedy within eighteen months but this day flaunting twin flags and a full complement of smiling faces, added a sprightly nautical flavour to the proceedings.

The pier, in those early days, was widely used for embarking on pleasure cruises. The North Channel provided a negotiable stretch of water for vessels of comparatively large tonnage, even at low tide, and many Blackpool steamers and privately owned yachts were moored within reach of the new pier.

By 1904 the pier had been widened and extended, and on the 2nd April of that year the Management had " great pleasure in announcing that the Handsome New Concert Pavilion, New Band Kiosk, and Pier Head Extensions will be thrown open to the Public and Residents . . . When a Grand Orchestral and Vocal Concert will be given in The New Moorish Pavilion." (Prices ranged from 1s. to 3s. 6d.).

St. Annes Pier showing the addition of the Moorish Pavilion and Floral Hall. (*Block kindly loaned by " Lytham Standàrd " Printing Co., Ltd.*).

The venture had cost . . . " not short of £30,000," and it was pointed out :

> " For this enormous outlay the Company and St. Annes . . . gets a most valuable addition to its attractions, and a cluster of over-sea buildings which is SECOND TO NONE on the coast . . . Storm and rain will be of no consequence ; visitors, instead of remaining indoors when the melancholy drip of the rain robs them of some of the pleasures of their holiday, will be able to get shelter where they will be capitally entertained . . . Internally or externally there is not one unsightly corner . . . The Ladies' room . . . is a dream of beauty . . . The Pier and pavilion will be brilliantly lighted by Sugg's high-pressure system . . . All the chairs and forms . . . have tip-up seats . . . No fewer than 1,000 persons can be seated . . . and panic bolts are provided . . . Shops are already let . . . there are public lavatories for both sexes . . . walls covered opalite . . . NO EXPENSE HAS BEEN SPARED . . .", etc.

At the same time, The Pier Plastic Performers, a new troupe of pierrots, were busy three times daily in the band kiosk presenting sketches and concerted numbers . . . " in what is hoped will prove an acceptable and distinctly refined Al Fresco Entertainment." (If wet, in the New Moorish Pavilion).

Walter P. Bell conducted open-air orchestral concerts, and George Burton's " Bohemian Minstrels " put forth a " melange of music, mimicry and refined wit." There were " animated pictures by the bioscope," and an open invitation to " come and hear the gramophone, the latest and best of talking machines."

In June, 1910, the Floral Hall, which had been designed by a former Mayor, the late Coun. A. England, was opened. There Miss Kate Earl and her twelve lady instrumentalists gave musical concerts for an admission charge of 1d.

Since that time, many of the great ones of vaudeville and opera have performed before audiences on St. Annes Pier. Denis Noble, Redvers Llewellyn, Leslie Henson, Ronald Frankau, Claude Hulbert, Avril Angers and, more recently, Russ Conway, spring instantly to the mind, and hosts of others, too multitudinous, as they say, to mention.

Up to very recent years, and in keeping with the conservative attitude of the original directors, neither advertising matter nor slot machines were allowed to spoil the dignity of the pier. Nowadays, however, much of the structure is covered, and never did pennies disappear so quickly as in the busy holiday atmosphere of this pleasure arcade which, above all, provides entertainment and shelter when the weather turns rough.

If some still sigh for the genteel past, perhaps it would be well for them also to remember that a great deal of money was locked up once which, at last, is bringing home its rewards.

THE LIFEBOAT MONUMENT

Perhaps few who take their holidays along this coast, or even live upon it, will realise that " Lifeboat Saturday " was born in the town of St. Annes.

In 1879 the St. Annes Branch of the Lifeboat Service was formed, and the first vessel brought into service was the " Laura Janet." Her crew was drawn from among the old fishing families. They knew the restless Ribble, they had matched the temper of her storms, and they were not unaware of the countless unnamed victims lying in as many unmarked graves along her shores.

Their Coxswain was William Johnson, and second in command was Charles Tims, a fisherman of great mettle and a famous man on this coast.

In 1884 this close-knit lifeboat fraternity gathered unto themselves a good friend in the person of Scots-born Charles Macara who had become a cotton magnate in Manchester. Mr. Macara (he was created a Baronet of the United Kingdom in 1911) had come to the new town, taken a house on the North Promenade, and instantly had become caught up in the affairs, and the affections, of this breed of Lancashire fishermen.

If he had come here to take a rest from the demands of a strenuous life, he was soon to become engaged in one of its severest labours. He loved these stout-hearted men of the sea. He liked nothing better than to accompany them at practice.

On 4th December 1886 a gale sprang up, and beneath the dark afternoon sky the crew of a small Montrose steamer, the " Yan Yean," were picked out from the shore, clinging to the mast of their vessel which had run foul of Salter's Bank. The "Laura Janet" went out and six lives were saved. From the Macara home the lifeboat's Coxswain and Sub-Coxswain telephoned their story to the Manchester press.

(*Photograph by Alderman A. F. Williamson, C.C.*).

But the storm, which had whetted the crew's appetite, had not blown itself out. Balked of its first victims, it now stalked fresh plunder, and five nights later, on 9th December, 1886, it hurled itself with renewed ferocity upon the " Mexico," a German barque bound from Hamburg to Liverpool, but which had run aground on the Horse Bank in the Ribble.

From three stations, Southport, Lytham, and St. Annes, the crews went out to the rescue. Flushed with recent victory, the " Laura Janet's " company were in high good spirits, though some said afterwards that Charles Tims had made ready with a thoughtful look. Maybe there was an ominous sound in this gale, a queer premonition of something not known before.

And so the boat went out, its single light winking and dipping in a welter of darkness. The watchers kept a vigil along the shore, and the womenfolk of the crew sought comfort at the Macara home. By dawn there was still no news, and in the grey light of day a horseman spotted a single lifeboat fighting to reach safety and shore. He galloped into the sea to meet it. It was the Lytham vessel with the " Mexico " crew safely aboard. Now it was for the same horseman to shatter hope and suspense and sow searing grief in their place. The St. Annes lifeboat had capsized with the loss of all hands. On the other side of the Ribble only two of the Southport crew managed to reach the shore alive.

This terrible disaster shook the English-speaking world, and none felt

92

the loss more keenly than Charles Macara. The lifeboatmen had been his personal friends. Their wives had looked to his own wife for consolation. Now it became a sacred duty to launch a public appeal which raised £33,000 in less than two weeks, and to stir the conscience of a nation to the needs of the lifeboat service.

The expenditure of the Royal National Lifeboat Institution, he discovered, was far above the regular contributions coming in from barely 25,000 of our large population. He made appeals, and more appeals, and great newspapers took up the strains. But in the end it was from the little man, with a copper to spare from his wage-packet, that the vital funds were to be drawn.

In October 1891, processions of lifeboats and reserve crews descended upon Manchester and relieved that warm-hearted city of its spare cash. In one day £5,500 had been raised in contrast to the usual £200 p.a. devoted to the movement. The idea of " Lifeboat Saturday " spread and within two years had become a feature of English life.

On this coast, meantime, the heroic self-sacrifice of thirteen men, and the grief of a whole community, had been commemorated forever in the monument, beautifully chiselled into the figure of a lifeboatman gazing out to the sea, which had been unveiled in 1888.

The doomed " Laura Janet " was replaced by the " Nora Royds," and even as the women wept for their lost sons and husbands, a new volunteer crew had sprung forth to take the place of the old.

Among them was the late Mr. Henry (Harry) Melling in whose house in Kilnhouse Lane I used to sit many hours taking notes whilst he turned up memories of the long past. On the morning of the disaster, though barely of age, and in direct opposition to his father's wishes, he signed up with the new crew and for long enough lived under the shadow of parental wrath. But the sea was in Harry Melling's blood. His ancestors were fishermen, one and all. He had put in one or two practices with the " Laura Janet " before her doom, and now he became a regular, under Tom Rimmer, later serving as Second-Coxswain for twenty years.

In the early days the crew received 5/-d. for a practice, 10/-d. for a day wreck, and £1 at night. Eventually the crew went on strike for more money, choosing the moment when the vessel was on the slipway, ready for a practice, to press their claim. From that moment their pay was raised to 7/6d. for a practice, £1 for a wreck by day, and 30/-d. at night.

After the death of Thomas Rimmer, Henry Melling was appointed Coxswain and served in that capacity for about six years, having charge of the " James Scarlett," the last of the lifeboats to be stationed at St. Annes.

Altogether he devoted 45 years of his life to the service. He was sand-grown ; he was a mine of information ; and he died, a few years ago, well on into his eighties, having given me hours of solid pleasure and a deep respect for our glorious men of the sea.

ST. ANNES—A TOWN BUILT ON GOLF

This " royal and ancient " game of Golf (introduced from Holland and named from the Dutch " kolf," meaning " club ") had become so popular, north of the border, during the 15th century, as seriously to interfere with the practise of archery. In 1457, the Scottish Parliament ordered . . . " That the fute-ball and golf be utterly cryit doun and nocht usit." Nevertheless, the pastime attracted more addicts until, in 1491, Scottish James IV, himself an ardent enthusiast, decreed that " in na place of the realme there be usit fute-ball, golfe, or uther sik unprofitabill sportis."

During the next three centuries, Scottish golf not only persisted, but drew many of our English monarchs northwards in pursuit of the game. Mary Stuart, within a few days of her husband's murder, was practising her shots at Seton. By 1608, golf was being played on the common at Black-heath, and James I had founded a club of convenience there for Scottish golfers living in London.

Many years were to elapse before golf could be said to have become indigenous to this country. The Old Manchester Golf Club, of which de-tails are elusive, was thought to have been founded in 1818, but inland golf at that period was said to have been " no more than a poor substitute for the real thing."

In 1864, the first of the seaside links, the Royal North Devon, was laid out for golf in England, and from that time onwards the game became widely adopted and was absorbed into the English way of life.

Perhaps no other single factor so boosted the development of the new town of St. Annes as this popular national sport for which nature had provided ample facilities (and hazards) along this coast. Indeed, for long years before the establishment of any Club, an exiled Scottish schoolmaster had been playing a lonely makeshift game in the sandhills of South Shore. Alexander Doleman, " The Father of Fylde Golf," had tried for years, entirely without success, to engage Blackpool's interest in the game. On this side of the boundary, however, there was keen and immediate response, and on 16th March, 1886, the Lytham and St. Annes Club was founded.

The club's headquarters were established at the St. Annes Hotel where, for many years after, the billiards room was known as the " Golf Room." A course was constructed adjoining the hotel, and the first tee stood at a point now covered by the railway station. Unfortunately for the golfers, the town grew fast, and the builder laid his greedy hand on green and fairway alike. Elbowed out of the way, the Lytham and St. Annes Club was obliged to shift to its present site where the clubhouse was built in 1898. Following the Open Championship held there in 1926, the royal pre-fix was added to the title, and the " Royal Lytham and St. Annes " sprang to its present fame.

In 1901 The Old Links was formed, taking over part of the course left behind by the Lytham and St. Annes Club. Neighbouring farmers, and the St. Annes Land and Building Company, were prepared to lease additional land provided that a nine-hole course was maintained for the artisans. Golfing circles at that time were knit by a truly democratic and family spirit, and the working man or the tradesman invariably pedalled to work with his golfing kit slung over his shoulder. This, one of the first clubs for artisans, was in existence until about 1928.

Meantime, largely at the instigation of Alexander Doleman, and on the site of Squire's Gate Camp, the Blackpool Golf Club was founded in 1894. It was a nine-hole course for the first eleven years of its existence, but it was extended to full size when additional land east of the railway was acquired in 1905. The two red brick houses which now face the camp served as the original clubhouse, but later a bungalow pavilion was brought into use, and this was used until 1939. In that year the aerodrome com-mandeered a large portion of the course, the pavilion was dismantled and re-built elsewhere, and the old Blackpool Club was scrubbed out of existence.

Part of their old course, however, was taken over by the St. Annes Old Links who were now able to extend to the full 18 holes.

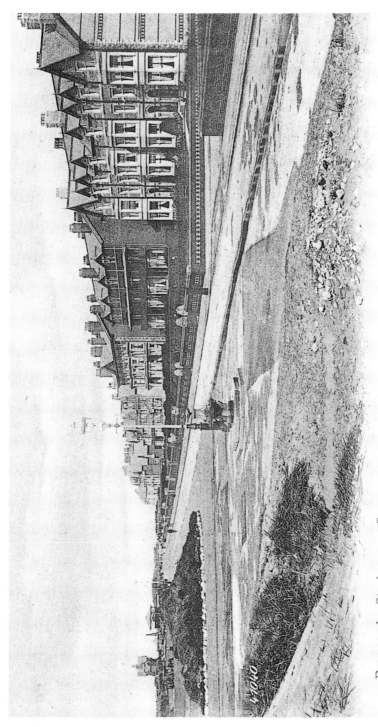

Promenade, St. Annes-on-Sea

Valentines Series

This view of South Promenade, at its junction with East Bank Road (where the Old Lifeboat House still stands, though with a different purpose today). The Victorian drinking fountain on the left is still there. This postcard was posted in July 1912 to Miss Daisy Wright, Rishworth, whose Auntie Ruth was '…spending my holiday here and having a fine time…a pretty place.'

Charter Day
Monday May 1st 1922.

This Certificate is to commemorate the granting by His Majesty King George V of a Charter dated the 28th day of March 1922 amalgamating and incorporating the Urban Districts of Lytham and St Annes-on-the-Sea into a Municipal Corporation to be named the Borough of Lytham St Annes.

C.F. Critchley. Charter Mayor.

Thornton-..., Deputy Charter Mayor.

D. ..., Charter Town Clerk.

F. A. ..., Deputy Charter Town Clerk.

Every school child received one of these certificates on Charter Day, 1922, along with a box of sweets.

In 1895 the Fairhaven Golf Club was brought into being. Half the 18-hole course was leased from The Squire, and the rest, bordering on the sea-front, from the Fairhaven Estate Company. Before long, however, there was an inundation of the sea which battered down the protective hulkings and submerged the original clubhouse (now the Fairhaven Lake Cafe) to the eaves. Household equipment, lockers, and golfing para-phernalia floated away in the flood, and a wooden notice board warning trespassers off the links had as much as it could manage to keep its nose above the water !

This chastening experience resulted in several holes along the shore being relinquished, and two adjoining houses in St. Paul's Avenue were taken over as new club headquarters. The course ranged along both sides of Clifton Drive until 1921 when the present site was leased and the Club settled down to a peaceful existence within the green and pleasant seclusion of Lytham Hall park.

The baby, and possibly the bonniest, of the Borough's golf courses, is the one which was laid out in 1913, bordering Lytham's famous Green Drive. The clubhouse started off modestly as a wooden hut, but in 1940 the bungalow pavilion of the Old Blackpool Club was carted from Squire's Gate and re-erected at Green Drive. Since that time thousands of golfers have travelled, often many miles, to play on this delightful tree-fringed and tranquil course which, though readily accessible, might for its quiet charm lie a hundred miles from traffic and crowds.

OUR HOSPITALS

The Cottage Hospital at Lytham was erected at the expense of The Squire, Col. John Talbot Clifton, and opened in 1871. It served all the inhabitants of the parish, and for long after 1875 it catered for the residents of St. Annes.

By the end of the First World War St. Annes still had no hospital to call its own. There had been a scheme, helped on by The Squire's generous offer of land on the corner of Headroomgate Road and Highbury Road, by which a Cottage Hospital was to have been erected in memory of King Edward VII. But war intervened, people were more intent on remembering their fallen heroes, and by 1920 plans were being laid for the building of a War Memorial Cottage Hospital. All the scheme lacked was money—an estimated £20,000 of it—of which the Committee at that time had only managed to raise about one quarter.

When subscription lists were published, more money flowed in, and to the £8,055 thus raised, Lord Ashton once more stepped in with the promise of £10,000.

Suddenly, a new development arose when " Banastre Holme," St. Annes Road East, the home of the late Mr. Thomas Bannister, came on the market. Building plans were hastily scrapped, and the imposing mansion, standing within a fair-sized garden and orchard, was purchased for con-version into hospital premises. Private efforts and charity events raised further sums, and by the time the building was ready to be opened, the total cost had reached £31,609, of which no less than £20,000 had been donated by Lord Ashton.

On Charter Day, 1st May, 1922, another, and certainly no less important, ceremony was performed when the Earl of Derby formally declared the War Memorial Hospital open.

AMALGAMATION

THE MARRIAGE OF TWO TOWNS

Having survived the storms centred around the first twenty five years of its existence, and having established itself as a gracious and elegant seaside resort, much favoured by well-to-do patrons, one wonders why the bobbish young town of St. Annes should have begun so early casting around for a partner.

In 1900 its leaders had tentatively dabbed at the idea of linking up with neighbouring Blackpool when that big boisterous town was seeking to become a County Borough. On this issue the adoptive " sandgrown 'uns " split into two opposing groups and for lack of support the scheme fell through.

In 1916 negotiations were re-opened. Once more, bouquet in hand, the suitor had turned up intent upon wooing his bride, and once more two highly vocal groups emerged, supporting or denouncing the merits of the union, and keeping the populace in a state of anxious excitement by means of public meetings, speeches for and against, and yards of propaganda in the local press.

In July 1916, following vigorous public debates, pamphlets were circulated, both by the Amalgamation Scheme supporters, and by the Members of the Opposition. A host of convincing arguments and comparative figures were presented to the ratepayers by both factions, and from this welter of conflicting evidence it must have been extremely difficult for the residents to decide whether they were likely to be better, or less well off, by linking their destiny with that of Big Brother Blackpool.

In 1917, a third pamphlet appeared, entitled " The Amalgamation Scheme Exposed ! " Adverse winds, obviously had begun to rustle through the negotiations !

They say it was the small matter of an orchestra playing in The Square, to the great enjoyment of the shopping crowds, which first halted the scheme's supporters in their headlong gallop. That, the Blackpool negotiators pointed out, would have to be sacrificed for a start. Otherwise North Shore would soon be pressing for a similar indulgence, and how long after that would South Shore be content to remain unserenaded ?

It was a small thing, a mere detail, but it was the first sobering glimpse of a steely fist enclosed within the velvet glove. Now, suddenly, the pride of the little town stiffened. Who was this lofty neighbour, anyway, who would promise us a Marine Lake . . . some time ! " We do not need Blackpool to build us a Marine Lake. We can do it for ourselves when we feel free to undertake the loan liability and put the profit into our own pockets," declared the Chairman of the Finance Committee. " We do not want a Marine Lake, nor anything else, one minute sooner than we can afford to pay for it ourselves."

It was as though the people of St. Annes suddenly realised for the first time that civic pride, personal sacrifice, and dauntless courage alone, had put their town on the map. They were independent and autonomous. Their finances, contrary to some insinuations, were healthy, and no problems were likely to arise which could not be overcome by exercising some of the robust confidence of the founders.

" We have home rule now, and we see no reason for parting with it," continued the Chairman, and a past Chairman, the late Mr. Edwin Cooper, summed up the situation most aptly in these words :

" I prefer to run my own business rather than take a big partner who would, in the course of a few years, whatever conditions were inserted in the agreement, run the concern for himself, and not for me."

These sentiments re-echoed through the town and the shutters were finally slammed upon any further mention of a link-up with Blackpool.

In 1918, a Committee of residents presented a petition to the Privy Council appealing for a Charter, enlarging upon the growth of the town since its foundation, and expressing the belief that a Charter of Incorporation would be " to the great advantage of the town by giving it a higher and more efficient form of local government . . . by fostering a civic spirit . . . and by giving . . . (it) . . . the additional dignity and influence which its history, its growing prosperity, and its enterprise, would appear to justify."

In 1920 it was privately hinted by the Clerk to the Privy Council that, in consideration of the smallness of the town, the petition might not succeed. What, however, were the possibilities of forming a partnership with neighbouring Lytham ?

Immediately, new amalgamation proposals were put forth, and once more not everyone was enamoured of the scheme, especially in Lytham itself. There were letters to the Press, public meetings, and representations made by interested bodies. On 31st March and 1st April, 1921, a Privy Council Inquiry was held at the Ansdell Institute.

Eventually (while the battle still raged privately in some quarters), the scheme went through, and the Charter, dated 31st March, 1922, was triumphantly brought back from London. Lytham St. Annes had now become a Municipal Borough with jurisdiction over 11,697 acres (including 5,902 acres of foreshore), and the Charter Day Celebrations would take place on the first of May.

May-day, 1922, therefore, must rank as the most important date in the history of this modern borough. Elaborate ceremonies had been arranged at points of public vantage so that everyone, especially the children, would carry lifelong memories of the occasion.

Unfortunately the weather turned awkward. Hundreds of umbrellas and scores of silk toppers streamed and glistened in the sullen downpour which scarcely let up throughout the day. At nine o'clock in the morning, St. Annes and Lytham officials, accompanied by our late Squire, Mrs. Clifton and their Agents, motored to the Warton boundary and presented the Charter over a rope barrier to Coun. Critchley, the Charter Mayor. Speeches were made and the motorcade re-formed and returned along the beach to the Lytham Council Offices before which a tidy crowd had assembled in the rain. There were more speeches, and a brass band, and bunting dripping dismally in the breeze. After the ceremony a signal from the lifeboat rocket called for a peal on the Parish Church bells.

The officials (30 to 40 car-loads of them) then proceeded in the direction of Blackpool and presented the Charter once more at the Squire's Gate boundary, and on the return journey were escorted into St. Annes Square by the local band.

Despite all the dampening effects of the weather, masses of residents, school children, ex-Service men and others turned out to make the best of the celebrations. The Charter Mayor sent a telegram to the King and

Mr. C. A. Myers (Deputy Charter Clerk) reading the Charter outside Lytham Council Offices.
(Block kindly loaned by " Lytham Standard" Printing Co. Ltd.).

98

The Charter Mayor, Coun. C. F. Critchley, J.P., C.C., presenting the Charter to the Deputy Mayor at the Lytham—Warton boundary. (*Block kindly loaned by " Lytham Standard " Printing Co. Ltd.*).

Queen, and in return received a message of felicitation from Their Majesties. There was a public reading of the Charter by the Town Clerk, a slap-up Charter Day luncheon laid on at the Grand Hotel, and another for the lesser officials at The County, Lytham.

This was May Day, 1922. The two towns had embarked upon a lifetime in double harness to a swelling chorus of loyal toasts. Now, almost forty years later, and despite periodic rumours of, talks about, and requests for " divorce," the two towns are still jogging along together pretty amiably, and by the exercise of good sense, tolerance and fairplay, the marriage should endure for all time.

FOR YOUR FURTHER INTEREST . . .

During my long years of research, I have read many books and used the work of many Lancashire scholars to supplement the word of mouth accounts drawn from our oldest inhabitants, and the many documents, papers, and souvenirs with which every locality is, or ought to be, blessed.

Sooner than inflict upon the reader a long list of titles which might seem burdensome, perhaps even terrifying, rather than helpful, it might with advantage be pointed out to the potential student how he may set about researching for himself.

Nowadays we of this Borough are extremely fortunate in our local history resources. At the Lancashire Record Office at Preston there lies an abundance of manuscript material awaiting our inspection. There are five publishing societies whose volumes will be found of help. The Historic Society of Lancashire and Cheshire, the Chetham Society, the Lancashire Parish Register Society, the Lancashire and Cheshire Antiquarian Society, and the Record Society of Lancashire and Cheshire.

On our own doorstep, the Fylde Historical Society centres its activities on the district, and in recent years the Workers' Educational Association has organised adult evening classes in Local History along this coast.

At the outset the student should resort to his local library. This Borough is fortunate in having two, one at Lytham, the other at St. Annes. Both have a fund of valuable reference material in addition to the books which can be taken out on loan. Once his needs have been made known he will be readily advised how to extend his knowledge.

The VICTORIA COUNTY HISTORY will be found useful ; A HISTORY OF THE RIBBLE NAVIGATION by Barron ; PLACE NAMES IN LANCASHIRE by E. Ekwall ; CLIFTON PAPERS by Cunliffe Shaw ; HISTORY OF THE FYLDE by Porter ; THE WINDMILL LAND SERIES by Allen Clarke ; A HISTORY OF LANCASHIRE by J. J. Bagley ; EVOLUTION OF A COASTLINE by Wm. Ashton ; OLD CATHOLIC LANCASHIRE by Dom Blundell ; THE APOSTLES OF FYLDE METHODISM by John Taylor ; SIR CHARLES W. MACARA, BART., by W. Haslam Mills ; HISTORY OF LYTHAM by Fishwick (Chetham Society publication) LYTHAM by T. A. Clarke ; LYTHAM by Ed. Ashton ; . . . THE HAYDOCK PAPERS by Gillow. Nor must one entirely overlook THE HISTORY OF LANCASHIRE by Baines, though much of his work and that of other 19th century historians has been put out of date by 20th century research.

KATHLEEN EYRE.